T0282917

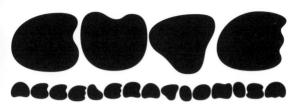

CUTE
ACCELERATIONISM

AMY IRELAND & MAYA B. KRONIC

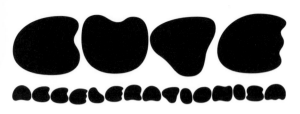

CUTE ACCELERATIONISM

AMY IRELAND & MAYA B. KRONIC

URB
ANO
MIC

Pobblished in 2024 by Urbanomic Media Ltd,
The Old Lemonade Factory, Windsor Quarry,
Falmouth TR11 3EX, United Kingdom

ISBN 978-1-915103-15-4

Distributed by The MIT Press, Cambridge, Massachusetts
and London, England

Typefaces: Riforma by NORM
             Meta Mascot by Formless Twins
             (Shangah Shin and Jaejin Ee)

Illustrations: 3, 9, 23, 29, 35, 41, 45 Maya B. Kronic

Printed and bound in the UK by Short Run Press

CUTE ACCELERATIONISM

Kawaiizome   3

Popstulates of Lingsquishtics   9

Topology of Bobbles   13

The Smol and the Epilated   15

Treats! Omnomnomadology: The Vore Machine   19

How Make Urself a UwU?   23

One or Several Catboys?   29

On Several Regimes of Lines   35

Fapparatus of Rapture   41

No Vanillas, or 'Cute Happened'   45

Notes   49

Bobbliography   195

Indeggs   211

Like blind men squishing a stuffed shark in the dark, many disciplinary discourses have attempted to feel out Cute, but the ulterior Thing remains obscure.

All transcendent explanation positions itself—'critically'—outside of its object, and by the same token expects that object to fall within a preestablished, coordinated, and controlled field of meaning.

Cute means nothing.

Zero.

For us, Cute arrived as a problem, an immanent encounter, a compulsion buffeting us up close to phenomena that made no sense and whose vectors pointed outside of all known coordinates. Cute is an Idea that can be known only through participation, a problematic object = XOXO.

KAWAIIZOME

Love, honor, and serve degeneracy wherever it surfaces.
William Burroughs[1]

The two of us rode cute/acc together. Or it rode us. Virtually at first, then actually. Cute teaches you what it means to traverse and be traversed.[2] We surrendered. We softened. We became rubberised and plushy, springloaded and squishable. Cute made us pliable with the promise of unknown pleasures, lured us with glimpses of a different meltdown in which, instead of portentous historical singularity and apocalypse, soft thresholds are continually dissolved by currents of joyful abandon. A future inhabited by furry planetoids, megaflumps, blobjects, and kitteh swarms rather than an endless doomscroll where the only characters left are Last Men: the gloom-mongering survivalist and the heroic shitlord truther. Maybe ever-acuter intensity doesn't logically entail ominous larping. Maybe everything's going to turn out okay. (Not naturally...and not for humans, obvs.)

All that is serious melts into Cute, because popping bubbles is the purest delight. In the beginning, cute/acc served as a frivolous deflation of the macho, grim, bossy, self-important rhetoric of contemporary accelerationism left and right alike,[3] and as a superficial 'joke' to mask passions whose irresistible pull invited the relinquishing of all caution and the disarming of all ego defence.[4] Was all that dark posturing just another way of stopping things from happening? What if we let go?[5]

We willingly assisted as it did its work on us, only to realise later that our friendship was flush to the fathomless surface of accelerating planetary cultural mutation. But that's how it goes sometimes. Acceleration is demonic. And demons don't tell you what to do, or what's going to happen next. They compel.

But if Cute is *already* about giving in—flattening yourself onto the desubjectivising flows of Capital's Moé-Conversion-Machinery, making yourself an (adorbs) object, asymptotically approaching the zero-point of submission and breedability...then Cute as an accelerationist stance is giving in to giving in (to...).

Cute opens a microcosmic gate onto the transcendental process of acceleration 'itself': escalating techno-mediatic plasticity of desiring-bodies hysterically coupled to economic and informational hyperfluidity in a diagram which, depending on what preexisting organic hidey-hole you are peeking out from, ends (you) in singularity sooner (than too soon) or later.[6]

Is the egg old or young, from before or after?[7] Neither left/acc progressive programmatic futurological civic planning nor anti-acc reactionary appeal to an imaginary past, cute/acc obeys the magical girl formula *acceleration = regression*[8]—a secret already discovered by those orphaned by postmodernity, those with no future and no investment in tradition, the swarming e-girls, t-girls, NEETS, anons, and *otaku* for whom the internet is level one. By nonchalantly operationalising accelerationism as memetic electrocute microculture, they have effectively extracted it from the double pincers of moral panic and academic buzzkill. Cute/acc is by and for those who have no interest in overcoming their passivity because Daddy Expects.

Throughout the derelicted warrens at the heart of yassness, feral youth cultures get off on allowing themselves to be invested by artificialised desires that migrate them out into new spaces of networked inhuman affect. 'Revolution is not duty, but surrender':[9] Go with what you want even and especially in spite of 'your' 'self'.

(Just ask Freddo: an awkward, sickly, socially isolated incel weighed down by generations of heavy *bratwurst-denken*, who still wanted to dance; sworn enemy of gravity, phil-LOL-ogist who called for a gae science, the first real theorist of the catboy; a child with lion's paws.)[10]

We are so over the self-important seriousness of lamenting the imminent loss of what is being torn apart, or of labouring under the delusion that we have a choice in how all its bits and pieces will be put back together again. Accelerationism is a mad love, a pact upheld with reckless integrity: submit to the future early enough to play a part in making it too late to turn back. Some don't return. Some come back scrambled. But everything that counts takes place before anyone can ask 'What happened?'.

The paradox of voluntary surrender to the inevitable is not a performative contradiction or a knock-down argument against accelerationism,[11] but the very topology of its anastrophic passion.[12] The backwash of anticipative intensity tugs you into the current so that whatever forms downstream will always have been inevitable. By definition, demonic possession happens before you know it, on a sliding scale, a telescopic ladder which transforms everything that descends it and therefore calls for magmatic lability rather than cold rigidity: 'There are movements for which one can only be a patient, but the patient in turn can only be a larva.'[13]

Anyone who has ever fallen in love gets it.

Determining the exact point at which personal responsibility melts into the transduction of demonic forces is a problem for sniffer dogs; accelerationists seek out slopes and get on one.

But which slope? L/acc, r/acc, u/acc, g/acc, bl/acc, e/acc, z/acc....[14] Channelling the restlessness of the terminally online into a perpetual feed of anticipative apocalypses, the pluralisation of accelerationism has revealed its fundamentally libidinal character.[15] The privileged entry points for participation in the future that each one prises open are so many indices of singular sensibilities or perversions, each of which radiates its own horizon. Precipitating it into an accelerationism is just a matter of sliding.

Which is to say, you get the accelerationism you deserve.

And we got the cute one.

Rather than choosing sides, steering L, R, U, G, B, E, or Z, we simped the demons, joined those with nothing 'better' to do, and became QTs. We continued to let it slide, now we are no longer ourselves, and no one can put us back together again. We have been reproportioned, made up, smoothed out, softened, epilated, multiplied, monstered—neotenised, moétivated, fashioned anew.

POPSTULATES OF LINGSQUISHTICS

Was heißt Cute?

Martin Kawaiidegger

'Must *a name mean something?'* asked Alice doubtfully.
Lewis Carroll, *Through the Looking-Glass*[16]

To scratch an itch properly, give it a name. Words make things appear distinctly, but things steer words obscurely. Addresses enable destiny. On the lip of the unrepresentable, Cute has been calling to an anonymous entity.

It's assembling itself out there, using whatever junk it can find (including ours), its diffident yet insistent booping of human culture tracked from inside history by a word as fresh and plastic as the syndrome it locates and cultivates. 'Cute' shifts along with the cultural phenomena it tags, snowballing the process and facilitating access as it tentatively hollows out a passage for the Thing that is pressing, finding points of ingress, soft-soaping its way in under cover of whatever feels good at the time, extruding itself into the socius.[17]

Keen to pin it down, we end up on the track of the irresistibly poignant. Following the etymological thread that passes through *acus* (Latin for 'needle' or 'pin')[18] we arrive at 'acute', which in Middle English becomes a qualifier for physical malaise, transferring the sharpness of an object of material culture onto the exquisite miseries of the organism,[19] thus presaging Cute's curious ability to bounce back and forth between objects and subjects, building self-propelling circuits of production and consumption, form and affect, that will later become the generators of an irrepressible cultural contagion.

The subsequent process via which the acute becomes cute is itself an *aegyo* cutification (or aphaeresis),[20] a diminution that not only trims the word to a stub but also initiates its shapeshifting between sharp and smooth, hard and soft. The eighteenth-century apostrophised form 'cute, meaning shrewd, keen, or clever, retains an unnerving and artful sharpness. But by the following century 'cute' begins to desert the realm of mental acuity to become a descriptor of on-point physical form: attractively neat, tidy, small, or compact by virtue of containment.

Thus packaged, 'cute' enters into the service of a nascent aesthetic sensitivity to the 'just-right' proportions of both natural and constructed artefacts[21]—a mode of appreciation and satisfaction for which, curiously, modernity required a term, despite already having 'beauty', 'grace', and the 'true' at its disposal.[22] Not a new word but a word for something new—after all, one searches the historical record in vain for cute pyramids, monuments, or cathedrals.[23]

Although it lingers on into the twentieth century as a byword for the smart and sassy, in the post-war years, homing in on an increasingly codified set of forms and qualities, Cute ceases to be merely a descriptor and becomes a factor of production in an expanding realm of synthetic objects, companions, and characters that artificially educe an indecent *excess* of just-right feeling.[24] Konrad Lorenz's discovery of the *Kindchenschema* and Nikolaas Tinbergen's ethology of the supernormal[25] retrospectively inscribe cuteness into nature while anticipating the collision of evolutionary biology and capital development, with the accelerated Darwinism of Mickey Mouse the (un)living proof.[26]

It has been arriving for centuries, and now it comes into its own, accelerated by a predominantly vision-configured global networked electronic culture[27] that cross-pollinates regional flowerings including the highly contagious shine of Japanese *kawaii*, kinder-scheming Korean aegyo, and budding Chinese *meng*.[28]

Having been subject to various regulatory mechanisms in force in different eras and among different sectors of society, Cute, in its obligingly squishy positivity, has tended to take on whatever characteristics are available—appearing now as insurance against the demise of the Oedipal status quo, now as titillating grotesquerie, now as aesthetic mode of the literary avant-garde, now as symptom of the postmodern evisceration of grand narratives, now as a form of political resistance, and so on, and so on.[29]

A needling suspicion remains: perhaps the apparent loss of reference to crafty intelligence is only a mask for some seriously cute moves. What could be shrewder than shifting attention from the fangs by growing the eyes?[30] Cute's 'lingering hint of wiliness'[31] is inseparable from our incomplete decipherment of its mission here on Earth. Despite the increasing codification of what falls under the label and its endemic circulation, replication, and contagion, *we do not yet know what Cute*—'the squirming word whose name means the shape it is',[32]—*can do*; its fascination as a sigint problem owes to the fact that, even while daily incanting its name, *cuuute cuuuute cuuuuute*,[33] a plunging dipthong punctually popped out by a plosive and all wrapped up by a tippety terminal stricture, we are still sounding out its latent shape.

TOPOLOGY OF BOBBLES

Cuddles have no interiority. Snuggling is penetration baffled by curves and declivities that teasingly deflect access.[34] Cute will remain cryptic so long as the phallus insists on continuing to view everything from its pushy, one-eyed perspective. Cute diffuses pulsions across agendaless surfaces that remain 'intact and unpenetrated (suggesting, in fact, that there is nothing at all inside)'.[35] Rendered more acute by obtuseness, full to bursting with sappiness but empty of sapience, the cute body is an invitation to edgeplay on an eggscape, a superpotentiated compact closed surface ('Impenetrability! That's what I say!').[36] An escalation that never amounts to anything serious, Cute is the protracted poignancy of the chronically inconsummate.[37]

All sincerity is rebuffed by this insouciant superficiality. The notion of an internal realm expressed with minimal mediation or distortion is reduced to a mere platitude: everything supposedly deep now flowers on a swollen superflatness,[38] and for the superficionado, there's nothing underneath. Cute is all-out or not at all.[39]

THE SMOL AND THE EPILATED

The cuddly cousin of asceticism and masochism, Cute runs a tangent to sex (or tangentialises it),[40] travelling near but always passing alongside.

Every drive is an OP Idea focused on a distant vanishing point the mirage of which, glimpsed beyond the closed circle it projects onto the looking glass of reproductive utility, serves to ensure that the organism overshoots to hit the target, tracking an extravagant vector that satisfaction expunges.

It is at the point where consummation is deviated and we pass beyond the looking glass that the adventure begins. Libido anticipates its own supernormalisation: OP drives include as integral machine parts multiple lines of flight that depart from the closed circle of the reproductive refrain.

If Cute's baby face gives rise to nurturing impulses, it simultaneously decouples them from reproductive, organic, ends. If it releases a rapacious gropitude, it simultaneously jellifies the aggressor into submisillybillyty.

Lorenz's 'releasers' can be supercharged to overtrigger fixed action patterns (FAPs) to the detriment of reproduction and even survival—particularly when supernormality is enabled by technological hyperplasticity.[41] Tinbergen's birds perched on their neon supersized clutch are no more likely to hatch a hale scion than the caveman in the mall munching his fourth Happy Meal® of the day.

Questions of fertility aside,[42] a drive satisfied is a drive that has lost its ideal dimension, in which dwells its potential for intensification, the shifting of coordinates, and the production of the new. Climax is arrested acceleration, but Cute is intensely anticlimactic.

> Intensity has no connection whatsoever with screwface PantoGoth male climax nor the cult of the Extreme Sensation. Rather intensity means the state of being in tension. [...] Being intense means staying on a plateau.[43]

Which is why, among the options on the character

select screen for contemporary eros, cuteness is the future—not hardcore transgression, softcore adulting, or reproductive tradsomeness.

Often described as an overwhelming or 'paradoxical' confusion of two highly invested vanishing points of desire, caretaking and aggression, Cute has been narrated as the weird tale of a flip-flop phenomenon combining the 'best' and 'worst' of the human animal, or occasioning their dialectical transformation: overdriven regulators clamping down on excessive feelings, overstimulated and then frustrated desires, care and protection overflowing into aggression and vice versa.[44] But these regulative mechanisms do not attest to the 'impossible' nature of the convergence:[45] on the contrary, they slavishly curtail its further intensification.[46]

'Torn between surrender and mastery',[47] in a 'confusion of drives' usually associated with feminine and masculine roles, Cute may have given cultural permission for women to be overcome by aggressive desire and for men to be disarmed by caretaking feelings. But only as a prelude to crossing the streams, activating a monstrous line of flight which owes as much to loving molestation as to aggressive protection,[48] and whose vector draws us outside the sphere of dimorphous sexuality altogether.

Supernormalised cuteness projects us into an acute angle where conflicting drives intersect, at an event horizon that continually recedes as it is approached. Cute law of attraction and contraction: the more you squeeze, the greater the chonk, the sappier the yearning. An event: To cute in the infinitive.

This condivergent positivity is related to the aggressively contumacious sweetness of the crush, defined by infinite attraction and lack of any internal knowledge of its object. *Squeeeeeeee* is a squeeze that never ends. A compressed target, the cute object is hypercompacted—a pink hole not a black one, neither virile nor fragile but infinitely robust. Regressing satiable drives to their insatiable Ideas, the truly cute is invariably *too* cute, ad infinitum.[49]

Does the angle between two drives have a happy ending? This is the question that the technocapital-enabled excesses of twenty-first-century Cute are finally homing in on. But 'cute/acc' is an acute pleonasm, since the capitalist process is itself one big squeeze. The constant deferral of a resolution between preservation and destruction is the condition of its continual intensification.[50]

Unbearable to the extent that it is actualised, Cute's essence countermands its existence, and the impossibility of its consummation renders those who desire it helpless, flailing, and cute in their turn.

On the other side of the hermaphroditic[51] vanishing point of opposable drives, beyond the comforting cadences of instinctual refrains,[52] Cute is an incubator of loves that are only just beginning to speak their name.

TREATS! OMNOMNOMADOLOGY: THE VORE MACHINE

[T]he ultimate index of an object's cuteness may be its edibility.

Sianne Ngai[53]

Even vore is cute/acc, so long as there's no chewing. Getting swallowed is just one big hypercuddle, and being digested by Capital's tungsten-carbide tummy[54] won't hurt.

Cute's affinity with compactness finds comfort in tight frames (which are just another kind of hug, after all). Hence the ubiquity of accoutrements such as bows, stockings, buttons, belts, and baby tees, all of which gently clasp the object (or subject), scrunching it into a little package, delivered safe and snug. Aegyo gestures[55] have a comparable function, framing the face in a manner that anticipates its reduction to a two-dimensional image, flat enough to slide into DMs. 'Cuteness has no inner world':[56] it bundles up by flattening out, subtracting roughness, complexity, detail, and depth—smooth and sugar-coated to go down easily.

'Even' vore? Or is eating the maximally extrapolated model? What's cuter, swallowing or being swallowed? Prey mode[57] or monster munch? Being inside something or having something inside you? Or both? Klein bottle,[58] Fortunatus's purse sewn the wrong way,[59] Duchamp's rrosy intertouching Bride[60]... post-hermaphroditic hyperconvolutions. Packaged up, entering into circulation, metabolised, slipping down the non-orientable surface of Cute, before long, the swallower turns out to be a swallowee. Ambrosia plague: Make yourself a good girldinner.[61]

As well as scrambling the coordinates of penetrative bellicosity and soft submission, Cute ultimately implies the melting of any polarity or distinction between having and being, possessive libido and self-objectification.[62] *Wants a cute gf -> is the cute gf.* It becomes impossible to consume without producing yourself as an object for consumption in turn. When fully unblocked, the spiralling Cute pipeline flumes l-l-libido from appreciation for cuteness to self-modification into a cute object and consumption of your own cuticity. Aegyophagy, autokawaiinophilia,[63] maximum cutagion density.

HOW MAKE URSELF A UWU?

It's obvious that the cat-ear phenomenon began with someone thinking 'I wonder what a cat would look like if it was a human?' Then all sorts of desires get wrapped up in that image.

Honda Toru[64]

'Doos oo always confuses two animals together?'
Bruno asked.

Lewis Carroll, *Sylvie and Bruno*[65]

Nothing comes more naturally to a cutie than making themselves up, and if you cute properly, you won't stay who you think you are.

It all begins with becoming-girl. But becomings are layered, one nestled tightly into another all the way down, and to pull on a skirt is already to begin to become a flower.[66]

'A man who would not accuse or depreciate existence, would he still be a man? Would he think like a man?'[67] A cute vanguard and the contemporary answer to Freddo's question, Femboy attacks Daddy Admin at the root, trading power for joy without a moment's hesitation, showing us how to let go, give in, and dress up for the future.

The skirtz gradient descends through a dense jungle of forking tributaries and unfolding vistas that never even offer the occasion to stop and look downriver at Man. Or, if so, only to see a pile of dust, since Man amounted to nothing more than desperately trying to stop anything from happening.

The next thing to go is the hands. 'If I wear paws on my hands, then their elements will enter into a new relation, resulting in the affect or becuting I seek.'[68] *Puiinng puiinng!* Anatomical aphaereisis: as the organic precursors of technicity are truncated, reiterating the movement from acute to 'cute, an artificial neoteny sprouts, with features of retarded somatic development along with unexpected dyschronic artefacts and new decoupages of the body: croptops, armwarmers, thigh-highs, fingerless hands, claws retracted leaving only paw beans, good for surrender.[69]

Not only is the front paw a deterritorialised hand,

the paw thus freed is itself deterritorialised in relation to the grasping and localised hand of monkeyflake.[70] Move and click, copypasta, post, like—pussycats can paw a mouse but can't type, so Cute is post-qwer as well as post-queer. ;lo0mkljobhjky78vhgt67cf56rxdws`` Challenger pads across the keyboard and through the strata, tail wagging behind. At each stage of the problem organs are uprooted, new becomings and new abstract-erotic stages unlocked. '[E]lective bodily zones' become targets for new 'drives which find in them a "source"'.[71] On the Möbius band of the great ephemeral skin[72] erogenous surfaces are expanded and transported, stretched and folded in ways that owe more to lateral transfer than to depthwise sublimation. (Is catboy tummy a nostalgic echo of the maternal belly or rather a libidinal surface grafted from interspecies snuggles?) *Papprrappaprrappa Ishukan Communication! Mantis with a radish....* The skirt machine is plugged into a paw machine is plugged into a stubby tentacle machine....

You will never overcome nature! The reactionary guard dogs bark. But which nature, that of biology as a 'rigid specialism'? Or an origami of 'lighthearted formulas' and 'humour' harbouring a 'presentiment of a certain kind of animal rhizome with aberrant paths of communication'?[73] In this matter, we have yet to advance much further than the polemic between the 'violent and serious Cuvier' and 'the sweet and subtle Geoffroy'.[74]

Sweet Saint-Hilaire understands[75] the plane of composition of nature machinically—in terms of materials[76] and their connections, not organs and their functions. There are no rigid sealed compartments, no arborifying branches, as in Cuvier, who traces his map of nature from the 'empirical distribution of differences and resemblances'.[77] According to Geoffroy's subtle and humorous diagram, all models of the animal are solutions to 'relations between differential elements', quasibiological particles beyond anything even the keenest microscope can discern...animal bodies are material results of the reciprocal determination of virtual, refunctionable organisational abstracta.[78] Cuvier won't have it: Geoffroy is 'more poet than observer', 'lacks logic from start to finish'.[79]

What time is Cute? All experience is chronotaxis, the accessing of time-deposits,[80] but the time that the individuated organism moves through—stitched together out of phylogenetic memories that are not its own—isn't that of Chronos. All animals can be virtually folded one into the other because they all belong to one and the same intensive plane. Actualised biology is not the model for nature but a funnel, a pet cone blocking our view of a vast field of transformative virtualities. Whales with teeth, zebras from the moon,[81] flying cassowaries, lion devouring a horse,[82] sex with anemone.... There are no ruptures, and transformations require not an impossible reverse back down the chronological timeline but a counteractualisation into the immanent egg.

> The egg is not regressive; on the contrary, it is perfectly contemporary, you always carry it with you as your own milieu of experimentation [...] Zero intensity as principle of production.[83]

'We're a little lost now.'[84] Is this a biological debate or a history lesson? But wait. Derangement of the senses, delirium, systematic recklessness, transcendental impatience—isn't accelerationism precisely this, the currency of partially deployed virtualities? Accelerationism is not futurological prognostication, any more than counteractualisation into virtuality is reversion to an earlier type. All is folding, becoming, production, construction, contagion, performance. And there is no freedom or exit from the process, only greater or lesser counteractualisations (the actual is the brake)— agonising, euphoric withdrawals from the drabness of the present-being to which you were allotted, awakenings, transformations, and infoldings, theriotypical swerves, 'strains and displacements which mobilise and compromise the whole body', 'systematic vital movements, torsions and drifts, that only the embryo can sustain: an adult would be torn apart by them'.[85] Don't grow up for God's sake, become the egg you already are, rediscover forgotten gradients, let the coordinates of your body slip off the surface of the world like so many half-sucked gummies. Twist, twirl, pop, sizzle, squish (if that's what you wanna do).

Strictly speaking, there is no outside (so there is no inside either), only as-yet-unrealised syntheses immanent to a process immune to exhaustion by mere personal biography. Rolled omelette.

ONE OR SEVERAL CATBOYS?

How stupid, you can't be one wolf, you're always eight or nine, six or seven.

Franny Deleuze[86]

Furries and femboys, *kemono* and *kemonomimi*, traps,[87] pups, and lemurs...'so many endlessly proliferating distinctions',[88] 'so many half-effaced or totally obliterated organs',[89] so many cuties!

To the Last Men spectating from the citadel, all of these transforms look delusional, infantile, and reprehensibly trivial. But everything that the Great Compact to Save Civilisation slates as degeneracy or barbarism smells like freshly baked mini muffins to us.

If 'the question is fundamentally that of the body',[90] this does not necessarily mean that Cute immediately calls for syringe and scalpel. The 'prison womb' will be experimentally counteractualised by all possible means:[91] 'Whatever it takes to access the plane.' The mother of '[n]ecessity trashes prohibition'.[92] It's not a matter of ripping off the face to reveal the gleaming technics beneath, or of terminating the body, as in the Male Fantasies of acceleration, whether condemnatory or celebratory. The stifling of the virtual body[93] in favour of the organo-social body can be intercepted effectively by all sorts of devices that operate collectively, releasing positive feedback effects.

'It is by a process of deliberation that the body begins to uncouple itself from its own and external authority.'[94] Even the most tentative re-rigging[95] produces novel proprioceptors, new relations between differential elements, reconfiguring the body-plan, piloting new affects, probing latent spaces. You don't need a mecha suit, a maid outfit will do. Catching currents like a transducer, the *shōjo* flutters like Albertine, *hirahira*, *fuwafuwa*[96]—the Spinozan spider's web of her petticoats catching elemental ruffles, cascading forces passing into and through her.

But this 'production is simultaneously consumption and a recording process'[97]—the broadcasting of these new forms of jouissance, their propagation and sharing, irreversibly mixing 'real' and 'fictional' imagos. If to be cute is to give up a certain mode of self-regard, it also involves viewing, liking, and sharing yourself as an object. The intense semiotic zones of social media potentiate cuteness to an unprecedented degree, accelerating a decades-long history of symbiosis between Cute and consumer culture.

Innumerable simulacra of impossible bodies circulate in the recombinatory matrix of the memosphere, massaging inchoate pulsions into shape, irrigating new thirsts, machining and distributing new partial objects, 'forming ephemeral syntaxes of hybrid cyber-circulation'.[98] And the larger the cute corps grows, the more soldiers of the egg (the only weapons they need are their curves), the more impossible it becomes for Daddy Admin to collapse any one individual back into their 'natural' body. So this is what they meant by *breedability*: a swarming.[99] 'Social media plague', but from the virus's point of view.

Initially popular among girls in their early teens, by the early eighties the kawaii aesthetic had become a means for young men and older women alike, even those who could not conceivably embody it 'in reality', to escape gendered social expectations and extend the tenuous freedom of a pre-social, pre-reproductive youth—the shōjo stage[100]—much to the chagrin and moral censure of 'mature' members of society and those whose subcultures were supposedly more 'sophisticated'.[101] 'The adults [...], being too deep, no longer understand....'[102] Daddy says that everything that goes on in your bedroom is delusion and degeneracy. Leave your fantasies behind. Be—be yourself—and be ashamed of yourself (all of which amount to the same thing).

But cuteness is acceleration. Discipline of enthusiasm, *schwärmerei*, contagion, and positive feedback...no one is inoculated.

Cute's unrealistic aspiration—meltdown into the egg—is simultaneously a pragmatic programme—patient dismantling of the sausage machine. In reality, the only fantasy you need to leave behind is that of a nonfictional, authentic self. Embarrassment, shame, and propriety all crumble before the allnicey onslaught of mass cuteness.

Snowballs and spirals, soft hacks and superpowers. Is it a question of escapism? Or rather escapology, actual escape rather than hedonistic dissociation from 'reality'?[103] Without the need for representation or organisation, collective desire drives demand for the production of new instruments to burrow ever deeper into the layers of so-called nature,[104] sucking up the germinal influx, nomming the cosmic aegyolk.[105] After all, '[d]reams are our eggs'.[106]

Be unyielding in your determination to make yourself soft. 'Very soft particles—but also very hard and obstinate, irreducible, indomitable.'[107] There are no rules: what feels cute now may need to be deleted later. To explore the virtual body is to break out from the prison of the flesh. To 'take back the body they stole from us in order to fabricate opposable organisms'.[108] Dimorphism and body-gender correspondence decline gently in favour of a navigation that is tactile, recursive, fictioning—a 'becoming' in the technical sense of a pragmatism-in-motion, this time rigged in your favour, 'a matter of careful engineering, the setting of scenes, the perfection of touch'.[109]

Since Cute has no interiority, it can't be about the attempted 'alignment' of one's body with a pre-existing 'inner self' or authentic identity. In this sweet torture, this awakening of a eepy dormant plasticity, becoming sufficiently powered-up to overcome one's lack of objective conformity to a spatial-proportional schema is a matter of artifice, and requires the production of devices for mediation, rigging—social, technical, sartorial, cosmetic, hormonal, genetic, molecular...but always collective. You never cutify alone. To cute—in the infinitive—is to swarm.

'We can go through so many bodies in each other.'[110]

Can confirm 🩶

ON SEVERAL REGIMES OF LINES

...all of the crushing assurance of this flattened being...

Tiqqun[111]

There are fundamentalists who have completely gone over to the two-dimensional world, for whom the chance of returning to the three-dimensional world is close to zero.

Morinaga Takuro[112]

The noblest are the flat animals.

Gilles Deleuze[113]

Saitō Tamaki's moécosmic theory of trauma[114] understands the history of anime as an iterated ramification of the inadequacy of standard human rationalisations of sex to cope with the experience of arousal by two-dimensional beings, and the replication, transmission, and refinement of 'drawn sexuality'[115] as a repetition compulsion driven by human culture's inability to assimilate *nijikon*, this enduring passion for the less-than-3D.

Now, anything appearing from the perspective of 'well-assimilated', healthily invested drives as 'perversion' is worthy of investigation. Against the *riajuu*'s insistence that affection for a fictional character is nothing more than the substitution of fantasy for reality[116]—a reality otherwise inaccessible to the misfits and outcasts who find *moé* in lines[117]—Saitō stands up for a new kind of desire: untimely, attuned to the alienating creativity of a world saturated with digital media, where almost every encounter passes by way of a two-dimensional image,[118] and following the contours of its own immanent principle.[119] It doesn't need to report back to the guardians of 'reality'.[120] It is powerful because it is self-sufficient ('I have no interest in three-dimensional women'), it doesn't give a damn about exclusive disjunctions ('I definitely felt something for Sapphire from *Princess Knight* [...] and Melmo from *Marvelous Melmo* [...] Sapphire is both a boy and a girl, and Melmo is both a child and an adult'), and no nuptial is too unnatural ('A train obviously cannot respond to these feelings, so we are talking about moé').[121] In the end it is Daddy Admin whose access is revoked, as moé's sheer indifference inverts the ontological priority, annexing reality to fiction by way of virtuality.[122] Between the 2D and the 3D 'there is this 2.5D, where reality is now being influenced by the otaku imagination'.[123] Flatline constructs: Pump down the volume.[124]

   This is a perfect way to approach Cute, because it shows how the emergence of supernormal cultural phenomena throws the coordinates of human sexuality into disarray and sets in motion a cyberpositive process.[125] Moé is incomplete burning.

   As Hiroki Azuma shows us, moé soon ceases to be about persons, even flat ones:

> As soon as the characters are created, they are broken up into elements, categorized, and registered to a database. If there is no appropriate classification, a new element or category simply will be added. [...] And then the elements [will reemerge] later as material for creating new characters.[126]

'Moé-elements' are partial objects that derive from fiction.[127] They are transposable, permutable, contingent, and repetitive. They can act as multipliers ('if you add cat ears to a girl then it *doubles* the cuteness'). And although they arise from the regime of the sign, their effects are always bodily.[128] Saggy socks, bells, cat ears, fluffy tails, antennae hair, maid costumes, *nya*-talk, a little fang, softness, smoothness, roundness, distractedness, sleepiness, a shy personality, a mysterious power.... Not 'simple fetish object[s]', but 'sign[s] that emerged through market principles',[129] the supernormal triggers of moé-elements plunder categories indiscriminately, mixing animal, vegetal, and machinic attributes and switching fluently between sensory domains. They are abstract, impersonal, and autonomous, immune to totalisation, and always in excess of the characters they define and the drives they serve to stimulate, breaking up into fragmented pulsions of anonymous desire the subjects of these drives in turn. After all, no one ever 'make[s] love with another person as a whole'.[130] Like the flash of red that compels the stickleback to attack, moé-elements are *releasers*, strange signs that do not signify, describe, or represent.[131]

Instead of a whole object of which they would constitute a part, behind the partial objects of moé there is only the 'database'.[132]

The database is the egg. There is no organisation inherent to it. It has no meaning in and of itself. *Yama nashi, ochi nashi, imi nashi.* As the ground of reconfigurability, the database can itself become the object of a libidinal investment just as powerful as those kindled by specific configurations of moé-elements.

But what does it mean to love a database?[133] To love a boy who is a flower that is a girl who is a cat that is a train…? To be lawless, inhuman, forever free to rearrange everything? To never have to think about which configuration came first or suffer the Anxiety of Influence, that grave and serious affliction belonging to another century and an altogether different sexuality? To be relieved once and for all of the heaviness of identity—which always resonates with the regulative, humanist, heterosexual grand narrative, even when subverting it? For everything will be dissolved once more in the furnace of moé-elements, logically antecedent but temporally simultaneous.

This is how moé teaches you the secrets of the egg. How many cute girls do you have to draw before you figure out how to become one? The otaku deterritorialises by forming an image, a tracing of the *waifu*.[134]

Dismantle identity and you dismantle guilt, fear, and shame,[135] so the desiring-cuteness of moé slips easily into auto-cutification.

> It's funny because I did try to do the whole 'hard align with femininity' thing even though calling myself a woman made me uncomfortable and I didn't feel like associating with that side of things but eventually switched to nb girl and then just 'girl that's past any human gender because I'm anime now'.[136]

Flatmaxxing for beginners: treat all consumable features of identity as partial objects and identity as a surface on which they can be placed, permuted, switched out, and rearranged. Take apart the gendered body and remix it with animal elements, plant elements, and machine elements. Proliferate posthuman anorganic alloys, 'revers[e], recombin[e] and reshap[e]' them in 'endless variations',[137] try out all the configs in the database, tear everything apart and put it together again, but always refuse to fold it all squarely back into the transcendent signifier of the self.[138]

Database sexuality is an immensely feminine sexuality, a sexuality without ego, a sexuality that has sex organs spread out everywhere—a sex that sociobiology cannot grasp. And because it is feminine, it follows that it is inhuman.[139] Moé 'is the true detachment from humanity, the final severance [...] a revolutionary vector', poised 'to infect the greater psychosphere as a transfem xenogender swarmmachine. There will be no survivors. There will be no resistance.'[140] Moétrauma is pure cutagion.

Now there is a plane, a languorous plateau. The peaks and the troughs have converged on a still sea, a silent ocean. They have found their limit and flattened out. Melting point.[141]

FAPPARATUS OF RAPTURE

The essence of cuteness is by no means anything cute.

Martin Egghider

We are propelled by disaster. We are moving swiftly.
What more is there to say? An aetiology, an etymology,
a symptomatology, an epidemiology, an account of
Cute's intrusion into human history, its disruption of
desire, subjectivity, sexuality, and bodies…. Nothing
uncute makes it out of the near future, and the cute
will very soon no longer be even remotely human.

It can't be a question of interpretation, since
there is no distance between it and us, but out of
curiosity, what are the last obstacles, the remaining
negative tasks of the immanent critique of Cute?

Enemies of Cute tirelessly attempt to belittle and diminish it. (Cute of them.) What are we to say to those who see only 'something like a correctable "mistake"', a consumerist snare or an evolutionary trap? Those who 'rid [them]selves easily of the idea that these are crimes, but less easily of the suspicion that they are fictions which, whether involuntary or self-indulgent, are useless, and which it would be better to dispel'. Those who call: 'Wake up, young people, from your illusory pleasures; strip off your disguises and recall that every one of you has a sex, a true sex'[142]—and a true sexuality, whether it is 'adult' and transgressive (in which case cuteness would be a childish, coy, timid, veiled, and inverted expression of it), reproductive (in which case cuteness would be both an evolutionary trap and a dubious neotenophilia), or authentic and free of objectification and commodification (in which case cuteness would be a cheap ditty, an artificial sweetener, an ideological manipulation).

A classic metaphysical error is in play here: the predominant accounts of cuteness understand it in terms of cute objects, or power differentials between subjects and objects, rather than an as-yet-unknown problematic X for which objects *and* subjects are vehicles or conduits. Cute is not a cute thing; cute objects may be trivial but cuting is not; the error consists in mistaking the product for the process.[143]

Whether the 'last instance' is evolutionary adaptation, economic infrastructure, or a firmly fixed

configuration of drives, Cute tends to be cast as a be-
guiling illusion spawned by an underlying real: nature,
capital, or the drives. Below the vivid but sterile surface of Cute lies the grey eminence whose reproduction is really being served by all this silliness.

Cultural critique views Cute as a product of alienation, an infantilising safe retreat in thrall to which
humans seduced by a 'false sensuality'[144] pour their
love into inanimate 'dead' objects, and at the limit take
on the characteristics of commodities themselves.[145]
Cute is located in the cute object, revealed to fall short
of the dynamic of genuine human relations.[146]

There are indeed 'stationary', 'dead', 'passive'
commodity objects. As it moves, any process of cultural intensification deposits in its path a cooling crust of
inert overproduction. But Cute arrested, placed on the
shelf and seen from a distance, can only be a parodic
residue of stalled participation in the process: a clinical
cutie 'produced as an entirely separate and independent entity'.[147] No-one ever glomped a funkopop. Understanding Cute in terms of existing objects, ownership,
and power, rather than as a transformative force[148]
that runs through subjects and objects, the critic satisfies their suspicions by ending up exactly where they
started.

Evolutionary psychology, hung up on reading all
human response patterns in terms of reproductive fitness, is equally inadequate.[149] Its only narrative and
time-axis is mating success or failure, which snips

down the speculative Ideas of desire to the size of their empirical consummation and its generative utility, and inevitably mistakes regression for degeneracy, dismissing everything outside the repro funnel as an 'erotic target location error'.[150] Its monomania even stretches to such comical turns as 'non-conceptive social benefits',[151] a last-ditch attempt to turn incorrigible traps to adaptive advantage. If it fails to shame you by telling you how bad your behaviour is for the species, this just-so whig biology will tell you that you were programmed to be good for the human race all along, in the best of all possible worlds.[152]

In popular accounts the two dovetail: 'the overwhelming presence of [...] supernormal triggers merely encourages greater [consumer] passivity'.[153] As if there were nothing on the other side of the looking glass....

Daddy Admin always wants to put Barbie back in the box. MRAs and Marxrocrats[154] unite against Cute, but Cute is elsewhere already.

Something is coming together here which only anastrophe can hope to grasp. Evolutionary triggers, ideological snares, and psychoanalytical drives are backstories, but only the future will make sense of what Cute will have been doing to us.

As a locus of cultural confusion, moral ambiguity, and critical dispute, as a phenomenon that irresistibly invites the question *What does it want from us?*, Cute must be treated as a pulsion unto itself, as glorious as it is mysterious.[155]

NO VANILLAS, OR 'CUTE HAPPENED'

Cutie is only
      the first touch of terror
            we can still bear
and it awes us so much
      because it coolly
            disdains to destroy us
Every single angel
      is terrible!

Rainer Maria Rilke, *Duino Elegies*[156]

But all of this only came afterwards. Falling in love brought us into cute/acc's forcefield, and it crinkled and crumpled and smooshed everything that went before, in a sweet tumble. Ubiquitous cuteness obsolesces macho rhetoric with irresistible positive circulation and diffuse passivity, melting you into its synthetic flows of lipgloss and boymilk, boba and baubles, candy and keratin. Doubling down on modding up, Cute is the pervermenon closest to the noumenon. Cute/acc doesn't care for Gnature or Truth, it is not sensible, serious, mature, macho, cold, dark, right or left, just soft, submissive, warm, snuggly, and utterly irrepressible.

Cute/acc signals endemic unseriousness, the generalised amorous intoxication of all social actors, fallen into a passion that is troubling because it discovers virtual connections by cutting the circuits of social reproduction ('Connect-I-cute!'). Making its appearance as the lowest, most abject form of surrender to sensibility, the power of Cute cannot be resisted by reason or the understanding.

Eggrything positive is contained in zero, and zero is immensely cute. 🐣

NOTES

Our 'little machine' operates at two speeds (at least).
'There is no difference between what a book talks
about and how it is made', and this one was lovingly
shaped by the amorous circumstances in which it
slowly blossomed. The main text, which we worked on
episodically over the course of four years, at first
trapped by COVID-19 on opposite sides of the planet,
eventually together, was originally commissioned by
the Melbourne-based journal Minority Report, but finally manifested itself as a performance-lecture (first
performed at Unsound Festival, Kraków, in October
2023). It aspires to the heavily-worked superficiality
and brightness of a hyperpop song, written to share
and intensify the exhilaration of our encounter with
each other and with cute/acc. Perhaps in the end it's
more of a dariacore monstrosity in which samples
from heterogeneous genres and obscure sources are
mashed up, distorted, sequenced (quantise writing!),
EQ'd, pitched up to chipmunk speed, and played off
against one another: a hyperdense chaosmotic hot
mess.

The endnotes, on the other hand, are a more
considered after-the-fact reconstruction of what was
thinking us as we struggled to make this song as cute
as it deserved to be. We recommend that the reader

*plays the main text at least once before entering
these obscure backrooms in which the sources of our
samples are documented, but which also house further elaborations, lengthy treatments of a number of
topics we had explored previously but which got
sucked into the gravity field of cute/acc, and provi-
sional answers to questions we felt obliged to work
through as the demon truly took hold and the irresistible force of this apparently lighthearted formulation
drew us further and further into its fathomless pink
hole.*

1.   As cited in G. Deleuze and F. Guattari, *A Thousand Plateaus*, tr. B. Massumi (Minneapolis: University
of Minnesota Press, 1987), 152. We choose to accept
as a gift of fate Brian Massumi's french-fried misback-
translation of Burroughs's actual advice on the correct
relationship to maintain with one's mania, faithful observation of which saw us through the writing of this
book: 'the only way to deal with it was to love, honor
and obey the madman when he was up'. W. Burroughs
Jr., *Speed* (Woodstock, NY: The Overlook Press, 1984),
46–47.

2.   According to sailor Gilles Grelet, for whom the
sea is a figure of the maximal refusal of the world, the
boat the minimal institution that makes it liveable, this
practice of sliding 'can be a crossing without exit only

because it is a twofold crossing, at once active and passive'. Its 'anti-erotics' consists in 'traversing while allowing oneself to be traversed' (G. Grelet, *Theory of the Solitary Sailor* [Falmouth: Urbanomic, 2022], 59). The consistent presence of a company of plushy *doudous* on board *Théoreme* must surely be the object of a companion volume, given their significant role in populating the sailor's solitude. (*Coucou, Magneau!*)

3.   For a history and prehistory of the divergent strains of accelerationism, see A. Avanessian and R. Mackay (eds.), *#accelerate: The Accelerationist Reader* (Falmouth and Berlin: Urbanomic/Merve, 2014).

4.   Blogging psuedoanalyst (*sic*) 'DC Barker' was one of the few to engage 'seriously' with cute/acc's first manifestations back in 2020, responding with an acute reading whose speculative reconstruction of the cute/acc primal scene was a factor in our decision to develop this text. Swiftly debunking the (absurd!) idea that cute/acc is 'merely an inside joke' fuelled by a 'flirtatious romance', Barker concludes that, as a counter to 'the stale, overly academic miserable L-Acc and the boring right-wing-talking-points-dressed-up-like-high-brow-theory R-Acc', cute/acc serves to 'undermin[e] [...] misguided seriousness' and induces us 'to return to the energy of crazed, dancing Nietzsche' and 'get back to "saying stupid shit" and "fucking around with the schizo-maniacal flow" as Guattari put

it.' <https://psuedoanalysis.blogspot.com/2020/08/
scattered-thoughts-on-cuteacc.html>.

5.   'Let Go' was the slogan of Unconditional Accelerationism (u/acc), which emerged in early 2017 as a
riposte to l/acc and r/acc, both of which it saw as mis-
guidedly promoting 'conditional' forms of accelerationism and thereby betraying a critical misunder-
standing of acceleration as a transcendental process.
See V. Garton, 'Unconditional Accelerationism as Antipraxis', *Cyclonotrope*, June 12, 2027, <https://cyclo-
notrope.wordpress.com/2017/06/12/unconditional-
accelerationism-as-antipraxis/>; E. Berger, 'Unconditional Acceleration and the Question Of Praxis: Some
Preliminary Thoughts', *Synthetic Zero*, March 28, 2017,
<https://syntheticzero.net/2017/ 03/28/uncondition-
al-acceleration-and-the-question-of-praxis-some-
preliminary-thoughts/>.

6.   A singularity is a point at which calculation of a
function no longer yields a tractable result, meaning
that information about the function prior to arrival at
that point is of strictly no use in predicting its future
behaviour. The association of accelerationism with
'The Singularity' is vague (referring to 'humanity' and
its inability to 'control' 'technology') and liable to pol-
lution by eschatology. Singularities, plural, are relative
to the various assemblages they irreversibly trans-
form.

7.   As dramatised by H.P. Lovecraft in *The Call of Cthulhu* and further explored in the works of Echidna Stillwell, the power of a mytheme may be gauged by its 'coincidental' emergence among different peoples and across disparate time periods.

The archetypal image of the cosmic egg, 'anthropocosmic, deriving at once from embryology and from cosmogony', has long been symbolically associated with initiation. In many cultures, the ordeal of an 'initiatory return to the embryonic state' is understood as a 'second birth', its model 'probably [...] the "twofold birth" of birds' (M. Eliade, *Rites and Symbols of Initiation*, tr. W.R. Trask [New York: Harper Colophon, 1958], 53–58; on the 'second birth', see also C. Kerslake, *Deleuze and the Unconscious* [London: Bloomsbury, 2007], 81–82). Buddhist imagery, for instance, describes spiritual rebirth as 'breaking the eggshell'; '[t]o break the envelope of the egg is equivalent [...] to breaking through Samsara [...] in other words, to transcending both cosmic Space and cyclical time'. The egg-cracking initiate defeats the 'obtuse self-sufficiency' of the profane, '"breaking through" individual, historical time' in order to achieve transformation and rebirth, in doing so rejoining the cosmic cycle of creation and destruction (M. Eliade, 'Time and Eternity in Indian Thought', in J. Campbell [ed.], *Man and Time: Papers from the Eranos Yearbooks* [Princeton, NJ: Princeton University Press, 1983], 173–90: 174–75).

If Deleuze systematically refuses throughout his work to distinguish between mythical and scientific employments of the figure of the egg, if he 'takes the esoteric dictum that the "world is an egg" unusually seriously' and returns to ovoid matters with ritualistic obsessiveness (Kerslake, *Deleuze and the Unconscious*, 48), it is in order to reestablish the theme as a device for initiation into a materialism of the virtual in which 'science makes mythology more concrete, and mythology makes science more vivid' (G. Deleuze, 'Desert Islands', in D. Lapoujade [ed.], *Desert Islands and Other Texts 1953–1974* [Los Angeles: Semiotext(e), 2004], 9–14; see also G. Deleuze, *Difference and Repetition*, tr. P. Patton [New York: Columbia University Press, 1994], 219–20; Deleuze quite obviously considers philosophy to be a kind of ovoid initiation-anamnesis; on Humpty Dumpty as Stoic symbol see G. Deleuze, *Logic of Sense*, tr. M. Lester and C. Stivale [London: Athlone, 1990], 142.) This enterprise involves drawing directly upon the work of those scientists who took embryology beyond the controversy between preformationism (the embryo results from the unfolding of a pre-formed seed) and epigenesis (the embryo is produced via the action upon a relatively homogeneous medium of internal regulative mechanisms, outside influences, or catalytic agents).

Von Baer (1792–1876) argued that the development of the embryo followed a progression from general to specific. But as became evident, the dynamic life of the embryo boasts a plasticity that sees it undergoing complex foldings and torsions 'beyond the limits of species, genus, order or class' (Deleuze, *Difference and Repetition*, 214–15, 249). Charles Manning Child (1869–1964; see Deleuze, *Difference and Repetition* 250; 'On Gilbert Simondon', in D. Lapoujade [ed.], *Desert Islands and Other Texts 1953–1974* [Los Angeles: Semiotext(e), 2004]: 86–89: 88) suggested that quantitative differences within the matter of the egg could sufficiently account for qualitative differences within the embryo, with axes, planes of symmetry, polarities and gradients that induced development resulting from the dominance of certain regions, attributable to disparities in 'metabolic rate'. In particular Child outlined how the development of organs depends upon an anterior-posterior 'axial gradient' of the organism between animal (active) and vegetal poles.

The work of Albert Dalcq (1893–1973; see especially Deleuze, *Difference and Repetition*, 250–52) belongs to a particularly sensitive moment in embryology just before the chemical and then molecular and genetic basis of induction was discovered. On the basis of extensive experimentation, Dalcq sets out an abstract theoretical groundwork for embryology. His redefinition of 'gradient' and field' (after Child, Gurswitch and Weiss), 'regulation', and 'threshold', along with the concept of 'morphological potential' (a measure of developmental plasticity to replace Child's 'metabolic rate') allows the induction of embryonic development to be explained in terms of 'topological characteristics, e.g. the relative positions of equipotential curves' (D. Thieffry, 'Rationalizing Early Embryogenesis in the 1930s: Albert Dalcq on Gradients and Fields', *Journal of the History of Biology* 34 [2001]: 149–181: 150–51, 170)—and this without the need for dedicated 'organisers' but only cascading stimuli and inductions (as remarked in G. Deleuze and F. Guattari, *Anti-Oedipus: Capitalism and Schizophrenia*, tr. R. Hurley, M. Seem, and H.R. Lane [Minneapolis: University of Minnesota Press, 1983], 355).

    Having rejected the idea that the material of the egg forms a 'mosaic' of immiscible zones with fixed destinies prefiguring the distribution of organs, and adopting a regulative model in which development relies upon positional gradients, Dalcq accepted that the material of the egg may 'embody some kind of spatial anisotropy while avoiding strict compartmentalization' (Thieffry, 'Rationalizing Early Embryogenesis', 170). There is no prefigurative map that resembles the divisions to come, but only a field of 'prestructural differences' (A. Dalcq, *Form and Causality in Early Development* [Cambridge: Cambridge University Press, 1938], 62). The 'initial morphogenetic movements' induced by differences in chemical fields and gradients when they reach a certain threshold 'lead to the juxtaposition or superposition of tissues characterized by different morphogenetic potentials' and a subsequent cascade of transformations (Thieffry, 'Rationalizing

Early Embryogenesis', 169–70). In Dalcq's model, 'kinetic activities which result from […] quantitative differences bring about a qualitative change' (A. Dalcq, *Introduction to General Embryology*, tr. J. Medawar [Oxford: Oxford University Press, 1957], 99–100), with differences in morphogenetic potential determining both the division into parts and their developing qualities, being 'at the origin of both future morphogenetic movements and functional differentiation'. So that, 'rather than making form and function dependent on each other, Dalcq intertwined these concepts by referring back to a common causal origin' (Thieffry, 'Rationalizing Early Embryogenesis', 170).

Differences in morphogenetic potential furnish a 'fate map' for the egg, but nothing intrinsically determines any local zone in advance, since its fate is inextricably bound up both with global spatial relations—'the fate of each part is changed, not by causes intrinsic to itself, but in dependence upon the new overall configuration. Indeed, 'this relationship to the whole […] is implied in the concept of "morphogenetic potential"' (Dalcq, *Introduction*, 90)—and with heterochrony: 'The gradually increasing complexity of the germinal system is bound up with the fact that certain parts […] may then manufacture more morphogenetically active substances. The other parts will be less well endowed and thus physiologically younger. A purely spatial map of the lines of isopotential is therefore impossible, for the time-dimension is also involved' (ibid., 91). Fate morphs along with its map.

This synthetic approach, reconciling 'the preliminary organization in the egg' with 'the kinetic aspects of its development and the ubiquity of regulative processes' (Thieffry, 'Rationalizing Early Embryogenesis', 157) undermines the strict duality between mosaic and regulative conceptions, and between preformationism and epigenesis (Dalcq himself says they are 'complementary' [Dalcq, *Introduction*, 7]—see Deleuze, *Difference and Repetition*, 251), thus 'disqualify[ing]' both extreme positions' (Thieffry, 'Rationalizing Early Embryogenesis', 171).

The dependency of Deleuze's embryological thinking upon the philosophy of Raymond Ruyer (Kerslake, *Deleuze and the Unconscious*, 63; J. Roffe, 'The Egg: Deleuze Between Darwin and Ruyer', in M.J. Bennett and T.S. Posteraro, *Deleuze and Evolutionary Theory* [Edinburgh: Edinburgh University Press, 2019], 42–58) seems to have been overstated. His direct reference on Dalcq's work, as well as exhibiting a 'high degree of fidelity to the source material' (G. Webster, 'The Metaphysics Science Needs: Deleuze's Naturalism', *European Journal of Philosophy* 2023: 1–27: 18), is strategic in so far as it focuses on a speculative moment in the science of embryology when an abstract general (topological) model was constructed in the absence of detailed knowledge of physical causation (but presciently so: the concept of morphogenetic field, whose influence had waned in embryology since the fifties, is today once again 'among the topics that excite developmental biologists' [H. Alexandre, 'Contribution of the Belgian School of Embryology to the Concept of Neural Induction by the Organizer', *International Journal of Developmental Biology* 45 (2001): 67–72: 69]). For Deleuze, Dalcq's model provides all the requisite elements from which to construct an ontogenetic model (the 'method of dramatisation') in which 'movement does not go from one actual term to another, nor from general to particular, but [...] from the virtual to its actualisation'. Beneath compartmentalisation and qualification, 'qualities and extensities', lie 'spatio-temporal dynamisms' which are the 'actualising, differenciating agents' that 'create a space and time peculiar to that which is actualised' (Deleuze, *Difference and Repetition*, 214); these dynamisms themselves arise from a 'field of individuation' or 'individuating difference' (ibid., 250) that exists prior to actual organisation, will be responsible for its determination, but bears no relationship of resemblance to it: the BwO, a map of intensity (defined by Kant as a one-dimensional quantitative variable), an implex of 'variations that are solely intensive, and that correspond to the internal zigzag of the Dogon egg' (Deleuze and Guattari, *Anti-Oedipus*, 154), 'crisscrossed with axes and thresholds, with latitudes and longitudes and geodesic lines, [...] gradients marking the transitions and the becomings' (ibid., 19) like Dalcq's 'lines of isopotential' which bring embryology into proximity to Leibnizian calculus with its differentiations and singularities (for an attempt to apply a general mathematical model of morphology to embryogenesis, see R. Thom, *Structural Stability and Morphogenesis*, tr. D.H. Fowler [Reading, MA: W.A. Benjamin, 1975], 29–31 and chapters 9 and 10).

In the world of myth, Dogon cosmogony as documented by Marcel Griaule and Germaine Dieterlen presents an elaborate account of the birth of the world from the cosmic egg. The 'descent and extension of the world' is schematised in a four-stage hierarchical typology of diagrams that prefigure Deleuze-Dalcq's embryological schema: *ideal field of difference–gradients and fields–spatio-temporal dynamisms—actualised form.*

The Dogon 'egg with signs' (M. Griaule and G. Dieterlen, *The Pale Fox*, tr. S.C. Infantino [Chino Valley, AZ: Continuum Foundation, 1986], 118) at first consists of 266 undifferentiated dots or dashes (*bummo*) which represent primordial essences, the ideal elements of Amma's thought. After this first series of abstract signs comes the seeding 'mark' (*yala*), which is 'like the beginning of the thing' (ibid., 33) expressing 'the future form of the thing represented' (ibid., 95). Next, the *tonu* (outline, sketch, foetus, germination) 'focuses on the organs or elements essential to that being': it includes 'its internal organs at the rough draft stage' and 'the "putting into place" of these elements' (ibid., 98). Finally there is the representational drawing, the *toymu* (the thing in its reality, the child) which now has a relation of *resemblance* to that which it will become in the profane world (ibid.), unlike the *bummo* which were autonomous, prior to, and independent of the things they produce ('the independence and autonomy of the sign in relation to the drawing representing the formed being are [...] emphasized' [ibid., 98]; 'the sign precedes the thing signified' [ibid., 92]).

　　In the first creation Amma had made the seed of the first plant from the substances of his own body, superposed the four elements, and made them spin. This creation did not hold together, however, and a second creation was achieved through blending, using the seed left over from the first creation, into which Amma had infused the four elements. With these primordial traces (the *bummo*), Amma first draws the marks (*yala*) of a new universe inside his 'egg' or 'womb' ('traced within himself the design of the world and of its extension' [ibid., 83]; the 'distribution of intensities' [Deleuze and Guattari, *A Thousand Plateaus*, 149]). After the *yala* of the egg, with its 266 abstract signs, in a second *yala* we see Amma's eye open into a star-shape *tonu* that prefigures the four cardinal directions of space ('permitting the recognition of the basic elements which give rise to the thing', Griaule and G. Dieterlen, *The Pale Fox*, 92; see ibid., 127). The seeds within the egg exit through the eye, spiralling, also becoming *tonu*, participating in the production of the space in which the *toymu* will be deployed, 'ejected', 'thrown into space to manifest things' (ibid., 88). Thus in a 'series of signs which repeat the successive stages of all Things' (ibid., 103), the entire cycle of existence is recalled with the progression from the *bummo* to the *toymu* which mark the budding of extensive development and by the same token 'the first step toward destruction' (ibid., 99).

In accordance with what Eliade describes as the mythical endeavour to 'abolish time [...] to efface the past [...] and to regenerate time by a series of rituals that in a sense reactualize the cosmogony' (Eliade, 'Time and Eternity', 174), the production of these drawings, a 'system of archives' (Griaule and Dieterlen, *The Pale Fox*, 100) itself constitutes a ritual reenactment of and social participation in the cosmic cycle of creation and destruction they schematise. 'The ritual execution of successive graphic designs is effectual and active: it promotes the existence of the thing represented, "re-edits" it by having it pass through its successive stages of formation' (ibid., 99). Drawing on this 'vast system of references in which all human activity is inscribed', '[i]n his gestures and speech man relives myth and it is precisely this reactualisation that makes techniques, institutions, and prayers effective' (M.P. Marti, *Les Dogons* [Paris: PUF, 1957], 56–57).

The hierarchy of diagrams also spans an esoteric-exoteric order: *bummo* are made by priests at the founding of an altar in a totemic sanctuary: 'the *abstract* sign, executed in a profane manner, but in secret (in the image of the "secret" of God's bosom where it was formed), is done for the initiate'; *toymu* may be drawn in common dwellings: 'the actual drawing, which all may see, is for the neophyte' (ibid., 100).

According to Eliade, myth never functions as conservative remembrance of primordial time; it serves to actively project into primordial time once more the human sick with chronology, confined to the mundane. Continual remembering reinserts Dogon society back into mythical egg-time, 'the contemporaneousness of a continually self-constructing Milieu' (Deleuze and Guattari, *A Thousand Plateaus*, 165), reinitiating all the cascading process that continually flow from virtual to actual by way of the complex series of 'transformations and elaborations' which the drawings depict (Griaule and Dieterlen, *The Pale Fox*, 92).

Furthermore, the diagram is immanent to the reality of the earthly cycles it both precedes and invokes: the *bummo* are drawn with *po pilu* grains laid out on the floor, and will eventually be swept away into the field when the rain falls: 'the drawing is washed by the rain, which "carries along (to the outside)" its form and force to "give it to man" and to promote that which it represents into reality' (ibid., 100).

The Dogon egg no less than Dalcq's embryology ('the embryo [...] functioning as a sketch', Deleuze, *Difference and Repetition*, 25), or indeed Geoffroy's anatomical philosophy (see note 78, p96ff) provides a model for 'dramatisation'. In both, '[t]he egg destroys the model of similitude' while revealing a dynamic which goes beyond any specific domain because it 'expresses something ideal' (ibid., 214, 250–51). And both feature time anomalies: like birds and snakes, initiates are said to be 'twice-born', making them in principle older than their uninitiated peers—but older in virtue of having regressed and passed through the egg (Eliade, 'Time and Eternity', 189; cf. Dalcq's concept of morphogenetic 'age' where less morphogenetically active = physiologically 'younger'; '[T]hough cute objects might appear childlike, it can be strikingly hard to say [...] whether they are young or old', S. May, *The Power of Cute* [Princeton, NJ: Princeton University Press, 2019], 7). The pluripotent egg before development, qua embodiment of undeveloped morphogenetic potential (the field of the Dogon *bummo*) exhibits 'the strict contemporaneousness of the adult, of the adult and the child, their map of comparative densities and intensities, and all of the variations on that map' (Deleuze and Guattari, *A Thousand Plateaus*, 164); it invites the would-be initiate to the amniotic anamnesis—both dis-organisation and re-membering—of an intensive 'past', a time which is 'not "before" the organism; it is adjacent to it and is continually in the process of constructing itself' (ibid., 164), a time accessed via induction into the embryonic state. Myth, inseparable from ritual, confers upon its participants the ability to access this immanent mode of non-chronological 'beforeness' in which everything participates, and to emerge from it transformed.

Although its origins are unclear, contemporary egg mythos (egg mode, egg_irl), referring to the cryptic manifestations of something (a chick, unnaturally?) that has not yet emerged from its latent state, or a future transformation anticipatorily evidenced by ostensible perplexity—exhibits a deep psychic complicity with the initiatory myth-complex and the ordeal of egg-time. Trans retcon even adds some exquisite anastrophic detail to the temporal anomalies of initiation, since '[o]ne only becomes an egg in retrospect, when one has hatched [...] an egg is displaced in time' (G. Lavery, 'Egg Theory's Early Style', *Transgender Studies Quarterly* 7:3 [2020]: 383–98: 384). Eliade remarks that initiation is 'equivalent to a basic change in existential condition; the novice emerges from his ordeal endowed with a totally different being from that which he possessed before his initiation; he has become *another*' (Eliade, *Rites and Symbols*, x). The 'temporal doubling' of 'a second puberty' (Lavery, 'Egg Theory's Early Style', 396)? At the same time, the second birth is what makes a 'man' recognisable to themselves and their social peers as a synthetic being of culture 'to the extent to which he is no longer a "natural man," to which he is made *a second time*, in obedience to a paradigmatic and transhuman canon [...]' (Eliade, *Rites and Symbols*, xiv). In this unnatural birth ('The initiatory new birth is not natural, though it is

sometimes expressed in obstetric symbols' [ibid.]),
the image of Man is washed away like a face drawn in
po pilu.

Re-edit the egg, but do not forget that this ordeal risks unleashing all kinds of disturbing participa-
tions. The great conflicts that take place within Amma's womb dramatise 'two lines, the one continuous
and germinal, but the other discontinuous and somatic' (Deleuze and Guattari, *Anti-Oedipus*, 155); the 'great
nocturnal memory of germinal filiation [...] in intensity',
filiation to the egg, is repressed by the constitution of
'a somatic system in extension' (ibid., 159). This 'system
in extension is born of the intensive conditions that
make it possible, but it reacts on them, cancels them,
represses them, and allows them no more than a
mythical expression' (ibid., 160). The mythical relationship to the egg initiates the individuated social being
into a secret: by way of the embryo and the placenta,
they are excestual legion, abruptly dislocated from the
time of lineage and succession: 'I am the son, and also
my mother's brother and my sister's husband and my
own Father.' For '[t]he BwO is precisely this intense
germen where there are not and cannot be either parents or children (organic representation)' (Deleuze and
Guattari, *A Thousand Plateaus*, 164).

From cracking open this anti-Oedipal secret, it
is only a small step to discovering filiations that are no
longer human. Which is why, for the neurotic Lovecraft,
hysterical dramatiser of his own ordeal, the mythical

time that erupts into the profane via the medium of those shamanic figures who, in *The Call of Cthulhu*, are able to dream dreams 'older than brooding Tyre, or the contemplative Sphinx, or garden-girdled Babylon'—gnarled redneck egg-timers who remember the old ways, or sensitive artists to which a time older than time speaks 'by moulding their dreams'—is not a wellspring of healing but an abyss of terror, something 'horribly remote and distinct from mankind' that 'I must not, and cannot think' (H.P. Lovecraft, 'The Call of Cthulhu', in *H.P. Lovecraft Omnibus 3: The Haunter of the Dark* [London: Voyager, 2000], 61–98: 65, 80, 72, 98). In the ordeal of the anamnesis of the egg, the dislocated New World poet's imagined affiliation to good olde-world stock strains under the pressure of terrible, twisted genealogies—not just 'nautical-looking negroes', 'mongoloids', and 'asiatic filth', but gill-men, betentacled cylinders, 'sea-soaked perversions' and the 'green, sticky spawn of the stars' (H.P. Lovecraft, 'Call of Cthulhu', 62; *Selected Letters 1925–1929*, ed. A. Derleth and D. Wandrei [Sauk City, WI: Arkham House, 1968], 68; 'Call of Cthulhu', 94, 95).... *Iä! Shub-niggurath! Spawn of the Dagon Egg, the Island that Rises from the Depths!* Surely this Thing has nothing in store for us but agony and eventual obliteration.... For those wary of crossing the threshold, embryonic initiation is a nightmare of consanguinity, sheer autoxenophobic horror. But the shamanic scribe is no more in control than the hapless characters beneath his quill and, with eldritch inevitability, the egg cracks and the cosmic cycle culminates in plushy cthulhus for all.

8.   'What regression brings to the surface certainly seems at first sight to be slime from the depths; but if one [...] refrains from passing judgment on the basis of a preconceived dogma, it will be found that this "slime" contains not merely incompatible and rejected remnants of everyday life, or inconvenient and objectionable tendencies, but also germs of new life and vital possibilities for the future' (C.G. Jung, cited in Kerslake, *Deleuze and the Unconscious*, 2). Slime or chrysalis goo?

9.   N. Land, 'Making it with Death: Remarks on Thanatos and Desiring-Production', in *Fanged Noumena* (Falmouth and New York: Urbanomic/Sequence Press, 2011), 261–87: 287; 'Revolutionaries often forget, or do not like to recognize, that one wants and makes revolution out of desire, not duty' (Deleuze and Guattari, *Anti-Oedipus*, 344).

10.   'Three metamorphoses of the spirit I name for you: how the spirit becomes a camel, and the camel a lion, and finally the lion a child.' F. Nietzsche, 'On the Three Metamorphoses', *Thus Spoke Zarathustra*, tr. A. Del Caro (Cambridge: Cambridge University Press, 2006), 16–17. #horsehugs

11.   See Ray Brassier's critique of accelerationism in Nick Land's work, <https://moskvax.wordpress.com/2010/09/30/accelerationism-ray-brassier/>.

12.   'Catastrophe is the past coming apart. Anastrophe is the future coming together. Seen from within history, divergence is reaching critical proportions. From the matrix, crisis is a convergence misinterpreted by mankind.' N. Land and S. Plant, 'Cyberpositive' [1994], in Avanessian and Mackay (eds.), *#accelerate*, 305–13: 305.

13.   Deleuze, *Difference and Repetition*, 118.

14.   Among these '/acc' offshoots and sub-brands are Nick Srnicek and Alex Williams's 'Manifesto for an Accelerationist Politics' (l/acc) in A. Avanessian and R. Mackay (eds.), *#accelerate: The Accelerationist Reader* (Falmouth and Berlin: Urbanomic/Merve, 2014), 347–362, as well as Laboria Cuboniks' 'Xenofeminism: A Politics for Alienation' (2015), <https://laboriacuboniks.net/manifesto/>; Vincent Garton and Edmund Berger's discussions on 'Unconditional Accelerationism' (u/acc), Garton, 'Unconditional Accelerationism as Antipraxis', *Cyclonotrope*, and E. Berger, 'Unconditional Acceleration and the Question Of Praxis: Some Preliminary Thoughts', *Synthetic Zero* (see note 5); n1x's 'Gender Acceleration: A Blackpaper' (g/acc), *Vast Abrupt* (October 2018), <https://vastabrupt.com/

2018/10/31/gender-acceleration/>); Aria Dean's 'Notes on Blacceleration' (bl/acc), *e-flux* 87 (December 2017), <https://www.e-flux.com/journal/87/169402/notes-on-blacceleration/>; and the recently hatched 'effective accelerationism' (e/acc) (see 'The Substack Sequence', *Effective Accelerationism*, March 2023, <https://www.effectiveacceleration.org/s/fywuJhWr-RmJZPhqky>). Meta-nomad's primer on 'zero accelerationism' (z/acc) rejects accelerationism as a fantasy that cannot be maintained in the face of global economic stagnation and imminent social collapse ('Z/Acc Primer', *jdemeta.net*, January 2019, <https://jdemeta.net/2019/01/11/z-acc-primer/>). R/acc emerged as a reaction against l/acc around 2017, and although it has frequently been invoked in memes and Twitter/X discourse, it has not yet been furnished with a founding text.

15.   Even the norm daddies can't help yielding to the pleasure of telling you what to do.

16.   L. Carroll, *Through the Looking-Glass, and What Alice Found There* (London: Macmillan, 1872), 115.

17.   'Its attempt at making its extrusion into this dimension kawaii rather than hentai has rendered the resulting agglomeration of eyes, tentacles and siphons far more unnameably challenging to the mind than if it had simply looked horrific.' R. Myers,

'Necronomicon', in *Proof of Work: Blockchain Provocations 2011–2021* (Falmouth: Urbanomic, 2022), 242–43: 242.

18. The French language retains '*aiguille*' for 'needle' and '*aiguiller*' for 'direct' or 'point'. *Acus* and related Latin words relating to pointedness, sharpness, high-pitched sounds, etc. are probably calques from the Greek ὀξύς (*oxus*), a word which covered a multimodal range of senses of 'sharp'/'keen' including visual brightness, shrill or piercing sounds, pungent flavours, sharp-wittedness, and rising pitch in speech (the acute accent, ὀξεῖα [*oxeîa*]).
 Cute thus 'embraces the sharpened, the pointed, the nimble, the discriminating, and the piercing' (J. Boyle and Wan-Chuan Kao, 'Introduction: The Time of the Child', in J. Boyle and Wan-Chuan Kao [eds.], *The Retro-Futurism of Cuteness* [Brooklyn, NY: Punctum, 2017], 17). Ironically (if not entirely incorrectly), Simon May insists that Cute is 'unpindownable'. May, *The Power of Cute*, 164.

19. *How now, oppa! how does thine ague?* In medicine, the Greek ὀξεῖα (*oxeîa*, see note 18 above) already applied to illnesses that are either shortlived or kill the patient swiftly. 'To be cute is to be in pain' (Boyle and Kao, 'Introduction', *The Retro-Futurism of Cuteness*, 17).

20.   A linguistic term denoting the loss of an unstressed initial syllable in the evolution of a word, from the Greek *aphaire-*: to truncate or take away.

21.   K. Waldman, 'The Totally Adorable History of Cute', *Slate*, February 2015, <https://slate.com/human-interest/2015/02/cute-etymology-and-history-from-sharp-keen-or-shrewd-to-charming-and-attractive.html>.

22.   'There were theories of "beauty" or "aesthetics" in ancient Western and Eastern schools of thought that sought to define aesthetics in general, ideal proportions, harmonious colors, and desirable relationships among parts. One can mention the works of Aristotle in Europe, Confucius in China, and Bharata Muni in India. Yet cuteness often features forms, sizes, angles, curves, and components that are not typical of classical, or even modern, forms of aesthetic "correctness"'. A. Marcus, M. Kurosu, X. Ma, A. Hashizume, 'Introduction' to *Cuteness Engineering: Designing Adorable Products and Services* (Cham: Springer, 2017), 2. 'Cuteness is neither the sublime nor the well-proportioned' (Boyle and Kao, 'Introduction', *The Retro-Futurism of Cuteness*, 17).

23.   'What about previous generations? What about previous millennia? Did prehistoric people produce cute artifacts?' (Marcus et al., 'Introduction' to

Cuteness Engineering, 1). 'Primitive' societies erected powerful monuments to their prevailing drives and the anxieties attached to them, yet none seem to have found the need to extol in their works the set of traits we identify as 'cute', despite their apparently instrumental and instinctively-felt link to biological and social reproduction: 'Not only is "cute" unknown before 1700, but Lorenz's *Kindchenschema* is largely absent from visual arts before the 20th century.' N. Steinberg, 'When Cuteness Comes of Age', *The New Republic*, 16 July 2016, <https://newrepublic.com/article/135244/cuteness-comes-age>.

24.   'When expressed in English, the concept of cute thus includes a fundamental ambivalence. In its definition of this word, the OED quotes two Aldous Huxley novels from the 1940s that include the phrase "indecently 'cute'": one referring to an affected French accent, the other to an overly dressed boy. Huxley's association of cuteness with an excess of feeling that runs beyond the bounds of decency is thus staged through pretense and artificiality.' J. Dale, 'The Appeal of the Cute Object: Desire, Domestication, and Agency', in J. Dale, J. Goggin, J. Leda, A. P. MacIntyre and D. Negra (eds.), *The Aesthetics and Affects of Cuteness* (New York and London: Routledge, 2017), 35-55: 37. Culturally speaking, the celebrated *Kindchenschema* is indeed a historical codification rather than a constant: 'In Italian illustration, a transition from the

miniaturization of the body of infantile figures and the emphasis of their gestures to an emphasis upon neonatal features (Antonio Rubino, Sergio Tofano, Gustavo Rosso) took place between the end of the nineteenth century and the beginning of the twentieth century. The historians of childhood literature Pino Boero and Carmine De Luca note that the adoption of Art Nouveau stylings in illustrations for children implied "features (which are) sometimes deformed and grotesque bordering upon the caricature of many characters."' G. Carpi, 'The Human in the Fetish of the Human. Cuteness in Futurist Cinema, Literature, and Visual Arts', in R. Catanese (ed.), *Futurist Cinema: Studies on Italian Avant-garde Film* (Amsterdam: Amsterdam University Press, 2017), 115–29.

25.   See R. Mackay, 'Hyperplastic Supernormal', in P. Rosenkranz, *Our Product* (Kassel and London: Fridericianum/Koenig Books, 2017), <https://readthis.wtf/writing/hyperplastic-supernormal/>. On the Kindchenschema see K. Lorenz, *Studies in Animal and Human Behaviour*, tr. R. Martin (Cambridge, MA: Harvard University Press, 2 vols., 1971), vol. 2, 155. It is important to note that, although reference to the Kindchenschema (including in Lorenz) generally emphasises its visual aspects, as Lorenz himself observes, '[g]enuine releasers can be found in all sensory fields—optical, acoustical and olfactory' (and, we would like to add, tactile) (ibid., 141). Our assumption is that study of

Cute at the level of human response would involve a multimodal integration and possibly an ideaesthetic approach. We also regard infant features as an *occasional cause* in relation to the ingress of the virtuality of Cute into the human sensorium. Hiroshi Nittono notes that 'infantility is not a necessary condition for the feeling of kawaii' (85) and is 'observed in affection towards babies and infants, but not limited to them' (91). (Hiroshi Nittono, 'The Two-layer Model of "Kawaii": A Behavioural Science Framework for Understanding Kawaii and Cuteness', *East Asian Journal of Popular Culture* 2:1 [2016]: 79–95). We therefore agree with Boyle and Kao that much writing has 'overprivileged the child in the affective economy of cuteness', and that '[t]he study of cuteness is [...] an investigation of the problematics of temporality' only in so far as it operates a derangement of chronology; '[t]he cute object may take the subject backward to the primal scene of trauma or forward to a postapocalyptic ruin' (Boyle and Kao, 'Introduction', *The Retro-Futurism of Cuteness*, 14). They go on to quote Thomas Lamarre on the children in Hayao Miyazaki's films: 'not so much about purity and innocence as about a sensory-motor openness, elasticity, and malleability. The child does not simply return you to the old pretechnological world but opens the possibility of a post-technological world' (ibid). Cute girls in transition, from heterochronic Ponyo ('revert! revert!') to shōjo Kiki.

26.   See S.J. Gould, 'A Biological Homage to Mickey Mouse', *Ecotone* 4:1–2 (2008), 333–40.

27.   Early computing's budding feminist economy of desire, stalled by the advent of the graphical user interface with its hand-screen-tool [...], enjoys a resurgence as software really gets gui in the age of social media. M. Fisher, 'Continuous Contact', *k-punk*, January 2005, <http://k-punk.org/continuous-contact/>.

28.   Meng (萌) literally means 'sprout', bringing the term into proximity with moé (see note 119, p144ff), and indeed the term emerged in online Chinese manga and anime fan communities from a reading of the Japanese 'moé' (萌え) in its Mandarin Chinese pronunciation. Released into the wider mediascape, 'meng' soon became 'a general exclamation for "cute!"' and was 'quickly compounded in new expressions such as *maimeng* (literally "to sell cuteness", to act cute), *mengwu* (cute thing), *mengdian* (cute selling point), widening the possibilities for its actual usage beyond the specific aesthetic appreciation of female pre-teen anime characters that the word originally refers to.' G. de Seta, '"Meng? It Just Means Cute": A Chinese Online Vernacular Term in Context', *M/C/ Journal* 17:2 (2014), <https://www.journal.media-culture.org.au/index.php/mcjournal/article/view/789>, in which the author negotiates the historical, cultural, and semantic dimensions of the term.

29.   Lori Merish, in 'Cuteness and Commodity Aesthetics: Tom Thumb and Shirley Temple' (in *Freakery: Cultural Spectacles of the Extraordinary Body*, ed. R. Garland-Thomson [New York: New York University Press, 1996], 185–203), argues that cuteness operated in late nineteenth and early twentieth century America as a tool of erotic regulation and social domestication, transforming 'transgressive [unsocialised, sexualised, and racialised] subjects into beloved objects' (194) via their induction into a benign realm of desexualised, depoliticised, conservative, consumerist familialism.

In *Cute, Quaint, Hungry and Romantic: The Aesthetics of Consumerism* (New York: Basic Books, 2000), Daniel Harris paints a picture of cuteness as a highly sexualised encounter with a pity-inducing grotesqueness, whose odd but addictive mix of protectiveness and excitement has us hooked on cute commodities: 'In light of the intense physicality of our response to their helpless torpor, our compulsive gropings even constitute something one might call cute sex or, in point of fact, given that one of the partners lies there groggy and catatonic, a kind of necrophilia, a neutered coupling consummated in our smothering embrace of a serenely motionless object incapable of reciprocating. [...] During the course of the twentieth century, the overwhelming urge to engage in cute sex profoundly affected the appearance of the teddy bear, whom toy manufacturers put on a rich diet, creating an irresistibly moon-faced dough boy whose corpulence invites caressing. [...] Pooh and Paddington have improved their posture, sprouted fat, dwarfish arms, and, moreover, submitted to a barrage of rhinoplastic amputations that has turned their crunching mandibles into harmless bulges that protrude only slightly from round, unthreatening faces. [...] Their arms are now permanently sewn in an outstretched position, rather than dangling at their sides as they once did, simulating an embrace as lifeless as the latex clasp of our "fantasy playmates'" (9–10). Always attentive to this duality, Harris's descriptions of cute objects are second to none.

Sianne Ngai explores the critical leverage cuteness gives to an analysis of the 'aggressively protect[ed]' (4) domain of formally compact avant-garde poetry with its 'unusually small lapidary, objectlike texts' (97) and partiality toward 'nondiscursive "twittering" or "babbling"' (98)—especially when it comes to picking apart the complex relationship developing throughout the twentieth century between the cultural status of the artwork and the cultural status of the commodity—in *Our Aesthetic Categories: Zany, Cute, Interesting* (Cambridge, MA: Harvard University Press, 2012).

Hiroki Azuma's *Otaku: Japan's Database Animals*, tr. J.E. Abel and Shion Kono (Minneapolis: University of Minnesota Press, 2009) reads the cultural circuitry of manga and anime production and consumption in late twentieth century Japan as uniquely expressive of the postmodern paradigm shift away from the modernist grand narrative, with its universalism, its appeals to originality and authenticity, and its function of ensuring social cohesion, toward a fragmented, collective, non-totalisable database structure that serves chiefly as a repository and distribution system for cute character traits (or moé-elements). See note 119, p144ff.

In 'Batman, Pandaman and the Blind Man: A Case Study in Social Change Memes and Internet Censorship in China', An Xiao Mina uses Ethan Zuckerman's 'Cute Cat Theory of Digital Activism' (which posits that cute memes and political activism typically constitute qualitatively different forms of contemporary online engagement, making it easy to identify and target undesirable political material) as a framework in which to demonstrate the ingenuity of Chinese internet users, who frequently combine the two in various complex ways to evade both algorithmic and human censors: '[I]n the face of stringent and targeted censorship, activists embed the activist message within the cute cat, within amateur media' (364). *Journal of Visual Culture* 13:3 (2014), 359–75.

30.   'It is not that far from cute to cunning' (M. Brzozowska-Brywczyńska, 'Monstrous/Cute: Notes on the Ambivalent Nature of Cuteness', in N. Scott [ed.], *Monsters and the Monstrous: Myths and Metaphors of Enduring Evil* [Leiden: Brill, 2007], 213–28: 214).

If we are talking strict quasiphonic particles (which of course we always are), the age of cute/acc is synonymous with the age of cat/acc ('or perhaps a rabid dog', E. Stillwell, 'The Vault of Murmurs', in Ccru, *Writings 1997–2003* [Falmouth and Shanghai: Urbanomic/Time Spiral, 2017], 65–71: 66). 'Something shattering is about to hatch' (Ccru, 'The Excruciation of Hummpa-Taddum', in Ccru, *Writings 1997–2003* [Falmouth and Shanghai: Urbanomic/Time Spiral, 2017], 97–99: 95).... As for the 'weaponisation of cuteness', we are aware that cuteness can be used as a ploy to sell, to exploit, to emotionally manipulate, to propagandise (for any cause—see Rose O'Neill's use of her Kewpie character to promote women's suffrage in the 1910s, for instance). Yes, we have also seen the TikTok cosplay troops. There is no doubt that cuteness, like any form of interpersonal human behaviour, can be used for typically human ingenious or nefarious ends. Our primary aim here is to consider the extent to which Cute's inhuman dynamic is repurposing human behaviour in ways that do not respond to preexisting or traditional human ends.

31.   Waldman, 'The Totally Adorable History of Cute'.

32.   Ccru, 'The Excruciation of Hummpa-Taddum', 97.

33.   Cute tends toward the inarticulate, since responses to cuteness when expressed verbally regress

speech to an infantile state, reducing it to emotive interjections, non-representational direct expressions of bodily affect which themselves mimic cute forms.

Japanese *burikko* (distinct from kawaii) involves a performance of overly sweet and infantile, coy and submissive behaviour patterns which prominently include vocal pitch and nonsense additions to language. Burikko is perhaps closer than kawaii to Korean aegyo [see note 55, p91ff] and Chinese *sajiao* (撒娇, lit. 'to scatter effeminacy', to be 'unrestrainedly coquettish'). See 'Amae (甘え) | Manja | Sajiao (撒娇)', Intercultural Word Sensei, <https://interculturalwordsensei.org/amae-甘え-manja-sajiao-撒娇/>; Hsin-I Sydney Yueh, 'Body Performance in Gendered Language: Deconstructing the Mandarin Term Sajiao in the Cultural Context of Taiwan', *Journal of Theories and Research in Education* 8:1 (2013), 159–82.

Burikko, sajiao and aegyo all involve various devices of stuttering, dearticulacy, and 'baby talk' (similar to the speech of Sylvie and Bruno in Carroll's pioneering work—see note 36, p82ff). Features of these performative modes also include referring to oneself in the third person, sing-song intonation, onomatopoeia, the addition of diminutives such as 'chan', and the repetition of syllables and addition of sentence-final particles ('la', 'ma'), etc. (see Yueh, 'Body Performance', 161). All appear to be designed to make the performer sound like a child whose command of language is incomplete, amounting to a lalanguistic 'reverse toward the abstract, pulling normal words back into their malleable infancy as preverbal sound' (F. Richard, 'Fifteen Theses on the Cute: A Crucial Absence', *Cabinet*, Fall 2001, <https://www.cabinetmagazine.org/issues/4/richard.php>).

At the limit Cute is too cute for words, and lovers caught in its billowing nets devolve into cutual muteness.

34.   Kawaii involves specific qualities, 'namely round, flat, simple, and smiling [...] Smoothness and roundness are preferred over shades and angles [...] simple contours are a determining factor [...] [T]he minimum requirement for something to be considered kawaii lies in its stylistic simplification, especially in terms of roundness'. K. Shiokawa, 'Cute but Deadly: Women and Violence in Japanese Comics', in J.A. Lent (ed.), *Themes and Issues in Asian Cartooning: Cute, Cheap, Mad, and Sexy* (Bowling Green, OH: Bowling Green State University Popular Press, 1999), 93–125: 97.

35.   Harris, *Cute, Quaint, Hungry and Romantic*, 20.

36.   Humpty Dumpty (Hummpa-Taddum), can(n)onical eggman and arche-grammatologist, 'master of language which, once descended, cracked and scrambled, lost its pronouns and couldn't be reaasembled' (M.B. Kronic, entry 'Egg' in 'Glossalalary' in E. Alliez with J.-C. Bonne, *Duchamp Looked At (From the*

Other Side)/Duchamp With (and Against) Lacan, tr. R. Mackay and M.B. Kronic [Falmouth: Urbanomic, 2022]), is one of the less obviously cute personae dreamed up by Lewis Carroll. For the Japanese, Alice, the most beloved creation of this alter-logician who adored little girls, 'embodies the idealised image of the "shōjo" […] who is situated between child and adult and is largely detached from the heterosexual economy' and thus free for all kinds of illogical escapades (M. Monden, 'Being Alice in Japan: Performing a Cute, "Girlish" Revolt', *Japan Forum* 26:2 [2014], 265–85: 265). Alice is 'flat and autonomous' and her 'aloofness and autonomy' is characteristic of the shōjo (ibid., 269).

Beyond the Alice books, Gilles Deleuze is possibly the only reader to have ever hailed Carroll's *Sylvie and Bruno* (London: Macmillan, 1889) as a 'masterpiece', casting aside the 'reservations and trifling criticisms' that have generally seen it cast as a laborious specimen of Victorian sentimentality (Deleuze, *Logic of Sense*, 43). There can be no doubt that *Sylvie and Bruno* is both pioneeringly cute and quintessentially Carrollian in its faithful and affectionate rendering of little Bruno's disarticulation of language, *which is a welly serious thing oo know*. '[I]t sometimes happens that a little boy is a stutterer and left-handed, and thus conquers sense […]. In *Sylvie and Bruno* it is the little boy who has the inventive role' (ibid., 13). Dodgson the untimely stuttering cutologist, Bruno the ungrammatical—the shōjo boy who has learned how to slide.

37.   In her exploration of the relationship between cuteness and asceticism, Elizabeth Howie suggests that cuteness makes desire more acute. 'Indulgence and Refusal: Cuteness, Asceticism, and the Aestheticization of Desire', in Boyle and Kao (eds.), *The Retro-Futurism of Cuteness*, 53–66.

38.   Takashi Murakami wonders whether '[t]he world of the future might be like Japan is today—super flat. Society, customs, art, culture: all are extremely two-dimensional' (T. Murakami, 'The Super Flat Manifesto', in *Superflat* [Tokyo: Madra, 2000], 5); in the same volume(!) Hiroki Azuma hails 'the leveling of high culture and subculture, the dissolving of borders between genres and the successive descent into irrelevance of existing learning and criticism—as a return to "zero"' (H. Azuma, 'Super Flat Speculation', ibid., 139–51: 139).

39.   'You can argue that, if you've read Liu Cixin's *Death's End*, the strategy of reducing your home planetary system down to two dimensions is a kind of "making yourself cute" in order to exit the "dark forest"—it's a defection from the game. The way to survive a dimensional attack is to do it to yourself first.' Rhea Myers, Cute Committee Meeting, September 2023.

40.   'By sex I mean the whole organic expression of our personalities in terms of our bodies and our responses to life. I think all kinds of intimate junctions

are going to be made between sex and technology, between life and technology, that will reverse the sort of logics that we accept today' (J.G. Ballard, *Extreme Metaphors: Interviews with J.G. Ballard 1967–2008*, ed. D. O'Hara and S. Sellars [New York: HarperCollins, 2012], 59). Amid numerous 'examples of a generalized degeneration of "natural" sex', today 'far stranger mutations wrack the sexual scene', presaging more clearly than ever 'the deregulation of the entire sexual economy' (S. Plant, 'Coming Across the Future', in J.B. Dixon and E. Cassidy [eds.], *Virtual Futures: Cyberotics, Technology, and Post-Human Pragmatism* [London and New York: Routledge, 1998], 39–47: 39).

41.   See Mackay, 'Hyperplastic Supernormal'.

42.   'The problem of comparison between animal and human sexuality consists of finding out how sexuality ceases to be a function and breaks its attachments to reproduction, for human sexuality interiorises the conditions of the production of phantasms.' Deleuze, *Difference and Repetition*, 250. Today, promoting the imperative of sexual reproduction is a social priority only for those whose chauvinism extends to demographic competition and the rivalry between 'races'. Meanwhile, '[t]he simulation of sex converges with [...] the corrosion of its links with reproduction, and the collapse of its specificity: sex disperses into drugs, trance, and dance possession; androgyny,

hermaphroditism, and transsexualism become increasingly perceptible [...]' (Plant, 'Coming Across the Future', 39). The productive forces of human sexuality greatly overflow the role they may play in reproductive function, fuelling acceleration and differentiation rather than supporting repetition of the same, especially when hyperplasticised and supernormalised. Therefore positive investment in the future cannot be the sole preserve of a 'reproductive futurism' that seeks a redemptive horizon in the reassurance of biological posterity. Such a conservative monopoly on futurity in the name of reproductive patrimony need not be mirrored in negative by a 'no-futurism' on the part of the queer lives it oppresses, nor countenanced by the parents of the children it consecrates, who—as will be the case for perhaps for a few generations more—have only delivered fresh bio-environments for memetic mutation, technohormonal experimentation, cute surrogacy, and AI pollination. Parents are not organisers but just stimuli, inducers (Deleuze and Guattari, *Anti-Oedipus*, 355; see note 7, p56). The rug rats are not interested in reiterating the sociohistorical infrastructure of Man. And then the ecto-uterine escape pods arrive.

43.   Fisher, 'Continuous Contact'; '[C]limax will always miss the cybernetic point, which is less a summit than a plateau.' Plant, 'Coming Across the Future', 39.

44.   "'We think it's about high positive-affect, an approach orientation and almost a sense of lost control," she said. "It's so adorable, it drives you crazy".' S. Ferro, 'Why Do We Want to Squeeze Cute Things?', *Popular Science*, 25 January 2013, <https://www.popsci.com/science/article/2013-01/science-says-adorable-animals-turn-us-aggressive/>. See also K.K.M. Stavropolous and L.A. Alba, "'It's So Cute I Could Crush It!" Understanding Neural Mechanisms of Cute Aggression', *Frontiers in Behavioral Neuroscience* 12 (2018).

45.   O.R. Aragón, M.S. Clark, R.L. Dyer, and J.A. Bargh, 'Dimorphous Expressions of Positive Emotion: Displays of Both Care and Aggression in Response to Cute Stimuli', *Psychological Science* 26:3 (2015): 259–73. Cute aggression, the authors postulate, 'may help to regulate emotions by balancing an overwhelmingly positive emotion with a negative response', like a kind of homeostatic cybernetic governor (negative feedback).

46.   It would come as no surprise to a linguist that Cute boasts this peculiar ability to combine opposing terms. The Greek word ὀξύς (*oxus*) from which 'cute' derives (see note 18, p71) is also the origin of the prefix *oxy-*, as in *oxymoron*, the conjunction of apparently contradictory terms. It is at this pointedly foolish juncture—*oxumōros* from ὀξύς, 'keen, pointed', μωρός, 'blunt, foolish', the word itself being an oxymoron and

therefore an autology—that cuteness (as Carroll so keenly intuited) converges with nonsense.

47.   S. Shin, 'Why Am I Torn Between Surrender and Mastery When it Comes to Cuteness?', *Some Archive #1* (Lucerne: Präsens Editionen, 2019).

48.   Ngai, *Our Aesthetic Categories*, 4.

49.   'Cuteness is perhaps the aesthetic threshold: "too cute" is a backhanded compliment.' Boyle and Kao, 'Introduction', *The Retro-Futurism of Cuteness*, 17.

50.   '[The] tendency to a falling rate of profit has no end, but reproduces itself while reproducing the factors that counteract it.' Deleuze and Guattari, *Anti-Oedipus*, 228; 'The tendency finds no end, the thing in motion never quite reaches what the immediate future has in store for it: it is endlessly delayed by accidents and deviations.' J.-J. Goux, quoted in ibid., 231.

51.   Cute may be seen as a hermaphroditic alchemical avatar, a mongrel cub of love and communication counteractualised by nymphoid desire. Born of the copulation between goddess of pleasure and passion Aphrodite and binder and connector Hermes, god of roads, cunning, and theft, raised in a cave by nymphs, Hermaphroditus enjoys a second birth when he merges with rebel naiad queen Selmacis—the rapacious

betentacled faunymph who gives her name to the fountain in Bodrum whose waters reputedly make men soft and effeminate ('Whoever comes to these fountains as a man, let him leave them half a man, and weaken suddenly at the touch of these waters').

Hanging there she twines round his head and feet and entangles his spreading wings in her coils. Or as ivy often interlaces tall tree trunks. Or as the cuttlefish holds the prey, it has surprised, underwater, wrapping its tentacles everywhere. [...] [T]hey were not two, but a two-fold form, so that they could not be called male or female, and seemed neither or either.' (Ovid, *Metamorphoses*, tr. A.S. Kline, 2000, IV:346–388, <https://www.poetryintranslation.com/PITBR/Latin/Metamorph4.php>.

Is this the vanishing point, then? '[E]very animal', as Étienne Geoffroy Saint-Hilaire suggests, 'was initially a hermaphrodite' (T.A. Appel, *The Cuvier-Geoffroy Debate: French Biology in the Decades Before Darwin* [New York and Oxford: Oxford University Press, 1987], 75). 'At the infinity of our loves, there is the original Hermaphrodite' (G. Deleuze, *Proust and Signs: The Complete Text*, tr. R. Howard [London: Athlone, 2000], 10). Certainly, hermaphroditism is an unavoidable staging-point in the future of love, regardless of whether or not you want to 'abolish' sexual dimorphism, since love can only be fully actualised in a situation where cuteness and being cuted is a symmetrical or generic operation. Unless artificially blocked, its double-impossibility inevitably implies a mutual hermaphroditisation. And '[w]ith the liberation of the double-sexed hermaphrodite [...] the gates are opened for the human being to become a libidinal microcosm, [...] symbol of [...] the 'Tantric Egg', or [...] the "body without organs"' (Kerslake, *Deleuze and the Unconscious*, 137; On the triadic egg and the double ['twin and bisexual'] body, see ibid., 135–37).

It is also true that Cute's 'erosion of borders is also reflected in the blurred gender of the many cute objects that appear hermaphroditic or indeterminate' (May, *The Power of Cute*, 7). And yet...don't we need to go beyond the primordial androgyne and the coincidence of opposites? It is the relation of Cute to surrogacy and cross-species alliances that disrupts filiatory lines, leaving Oedipus in the dust, and reveals the true extent of its transdiagonality. 'Fragmentation leads us to a theory of novelty where we do not need to understand each piece or fragment as part of an ancient whole [...] the theory of heterogenesis [...] is not a theory of the unity of the sexes.' A. Sauvagnargues, 'The Wasp and the Orchid', in P. de Assis and P. Guidici (eds.), *Aberrant Nuptials: Deleuze and Artistic Research 2* (Leuven: Leuven University Press, 2019), 177–82: 178.

52.   It was Ballard who taught us that the atonal symphonies the postmodern media environment plays on our neurons cannot possibly be understood

in terms of classical tonality (nor are they well-tempered).

53.   Ngai, *Our Aesthetic Categories*, 79.

54.   J.F. Lyotard, 'Desirevolution', in Avanessian and Mackay (eds.), *#accelerate*, 243–47: 244; 'Look out! It's eating everything in its path!' I.H. Grant, 'Black Ice', in J.B. Dixon and E. Cassidy (eds.), *Virtual Futures: Cyberotics, Technology, and Post-Human Pragmatism* (London and New York: Routledge, 1998), 132–43: 132.

55.   Aegyo is an exaggerated performance of winsome petulance that became a cultural phenomenon in Korea in the 2000s, connected to the rise of K-Pop and idol culture. It involves the use of overly sweet baby-talk and infantile mannerisms to get one's way, along with a set of conventional gestures, some of which mimic emojis, and a number of cosmetic facial cues including puffiness beneath the eyes (*aegyo sal*). Although ostensibly manipulative in intent, aegyo incorporates a consciousness of its artificiality on the part of both performer and audience, along with a keen awareness that even successful aegyo is only ever a moment away from collapsing into cringey ingratiating behaviour; the probing of this limit of Cute is part of the performance, as can be seen clearly in aegyo battles on TV shows such as *Weekly Idol*, in which competitors attempt to charm their peers.

In common with many manifestations of Cute, aegyo, originally highly female-coded, has gradually drifted from its gendered origins. (See also note 30, p80 on speech.)

56. 'What Makes Something Cute?: Cute vs Kawaii', *Slap Happy Larry*, January 2023, <https://www.slap-happylarry.com/cute-definition-cute-vs-kawaii/>. Even 3D cute characters are really 2D carapaces, eggshells without ghosts. Cut them open and they don't bleed, but only reveal smooth flat cross-sectional planes of viscera which can be sliced again and again without ever yielding the elusive dimension of depth. On the other hand, Alex Quicho has suggested that, since cuteness is not a physical quality but something that is 'laminated' onto the body, so that cuteness has a natural affinity with the world of avatars and skins (Cute Committee Meeting, September 2023).

57. See A. Quicho, 'Prey Mode: Why Girls are Pretending to be Cute Animals Online', *Dazed Digital*, 20 November 2023, <https://www.dazeddigital.com/life-culture/article/61336/1/going-prey-mode-girls-cute-animals-online-canthal-tilt-tiktok>.

58. That 'divine bottle' which harbours a disquieting strangeness 'in its orifice [*dans la cul*]': 'not just anyone can do this, drawing your lining out through your neck'! J. Lacan, 'Problèmes cruciaux pour la psychanalyse.

Compte rendu du séminaire 1964–1965', in *Autres Écrits* (Paris: Seuil, 2001), 199–202.

59.   'Whatever is *inside* that Purse, is *outside* it; and whatever is *outside* it, is *inside* it.' L. Carroll, *Sylvie and Bruno Concluded* (London: Macmillan, 1893), 104; for sewing instructions, 101–2; see Deleuze, *Logic of Sense*, 11.

60.   'The only serious thing I can consider is eroticism [...] And I have tried to use it as a platform for *The Bride* [...]. This idea is an old idea of mine, explained by the fact that a tactile sensation that envelopes all sides of an object "approaches" a four-dimensional tactile sensation—Because, of course, none of our senses have any four-dimensional application, except perhaps for touch, and therefore the act of love as a tactile sublimation could allow us to glimpse or rather to intertouch [*entretoucher*] a physical interpretation of the fourth dimension.' Cited in A. Jouffroy, *Marcel Duchamp* (Paris: Centre Pompidou/Dumerchez, 1997), 40. On the link between Duchamp's 4D erotics and Rrose Sélavy's genderfuckery, see É. Alliez with J-.C. Bonne, *Duchamp Looked At (From the Other Side)/ Duchamp With (and Against) Lacan*, tr. R. Mackay and M.B. Kronic (Falmouth: Urbanomic, 2022).

61.   See R. Negarestani, 'A Good Meal', in *Abducting the Outside: Collected Writings 2003–2018* (Falmouth

and New York: Urbanomic/Sequence Press, 2024).

62.   'Conflating desire with identification, or "wanting to have" with "wanting to be or be like", the experience of cuteness thus produces a "strange constriction of the gap between consumer and commodity", a shrinking of the distance that, like the affect of empathy which indexes it, is strongly aligned with the feminine.' Shin, 'Why am I Torn Between Surrender and Mastery'. This process is endemic to the third circuit of acutification—see note 155, p186ff.

63.   Another crumbling bastion of repression, the shaming of autophilias is literally nothing more or less than a prohibition on enjoying yourself.

64.   T. Honda, 'The Love Revolution is Here', in P.W. Galbraith (ed.), *The Moé Manifesto*, 117–25: 121.

65.   Carroll, *Sylvie and Bruno*, 130.

66.   Upside-down though, and what can you make of blooms whose petals go spinny and whose stamen are offered secretly to the earth instead of yearning for the sun?

67.   G. Deleuze, *Nietzsche and Philosophy*, tr. H. Tomlinson (London and New York: Continuum, 2002), 35.

68.   Deleuze and Guattari, *A Thousand Plateaus*, 258.

69.   There is a reason why 'kittens' rhymes with 'mittens'. Fingers—and even toes—are an embarrassment to Cute because they *see* too much. Cute is indifferent to discerning high-res manipulations, it requires all extremities to be eroded into nubby nuzzlers. The 'limbs of the cute are stubby or nonexistent' (Richard, 'Fifteen Theses'); kawaii fashion dolls have 'rounded (if not stumpy) features' (Shiokawa, 'Cute But Deadly', 96); Sleek, elongated American cars are too 'angry' and therefore *kawaikunai* (ibid., 96–97). Cute is pointedly blunt (or oxymoronic—see note 46, p87ff), it playbites without teethmarks, embraces without grasping, and deflects every poke into a glissade. (As for painted nails, isn't their function precisely to ridicule and sissify the indexical orientation of all-too-clever fingers in much the same way that cutespeak renders language ridiculous? A twofold humiiliation of hominid articulacy worthy of Barker.)

70.   Ibid., 61.

71.   Deleuze, *Logic of Sense*, 225.

72.   See J.-F. Lyotard, *Libidinal Economy*, tr. I.H. Grant (Bloomington and Indianapolis: Indiana University Press, 1993).

73.   Deleuze and Guattari, *A Thousand Plateaus*, 47.

74.   Ibid.

75.   'Knowledge is so sweet when one has arrived at a series of deductions which appear to the mind with the character of a perfect lucidity.' Geoffroy, cited in Appel, *The Cuvier-Geoffroy Debate*, 78.

76.   'Geoffroy's theory was thoroughly materialistic' and 'absorbed the vision of the Laplacian program without any of the discipline'. Ibid., 79.

77.   Deleuze, *Difference and Repetition*, 184.

78.   'I seek the ways and means of the metamorphosis of organs' (É. Geoffroy Saint-Hilaire, *Études progressives d'un naturaliste* [Paris: Roret, 1835], 107). This dispute is a matter of fundamental philosophical orientation and method. With plasticity and continuity as guiding hypotheses and homology privileged over function (see Appel, *The Cuvier-Geoffroy Debate*, 69–71), Geoffroy replaces comparative anatomy with an anatomical philosophy or philosophical anatomy (see ibid., 98) for which there is only one great transcendental animal.
        While, as Cuvier assiduously pointed out (see Appel, *The Cuvier-Geoffroy Debate*, 91), the idea that all animals share a basic common body-plan was not

a new one (having been advanced by Aristotle, Leonardo da Vinci, and Newton among others; see T. Cahn, *La Vie et l'œuvre d'Étienne Geoffroy Saint-Hilaire* [Paris: PUF, 1962], 12), in his definition of this unified plan(e) Geoffroy departed from the mere observation and cataloguing of similarities: he raised unity of composition to the level of a transcendental principle, and enthusiastically multiplied interspecies continuities and homologies (or what he called 'analogies').

'A confused kind of pantheism is hidden behind your theory of analogs', Cuvier objects (E. Perrier, *The Philosophy of Zoology Before Darwin*, tr. A. McBirney [Dordrecht: Springer, 2009], 109). And Cuvier was quite right to accuse Geoffroy of stubbornly maintaining a principle which no amount of factual gradgrinding could ever yield. But '[t]he Muse did not allow him to settle for half a solution', and, empirically justifiable or not, it was the 'alluring phantom' (ibid., 75) of the unified plan(e) of composition that enabled the visionary naturalist to open up new paths for the biological sciences.

That is not to say that Geoffroy had no time for the empirical: like a geologist examining the rocky outcrops of strata, certain that even abrupt variations can be accommodated within a uniformitarian regime of transformations and foldings, Geoffroy begins by seeking out salient points of difference between empirical features which reveal the lineaments of underlying virtual continuities (e.g. the ostrich's wishbone and the human shoulder-bone). In this first stage he proceeds 'geometrically', as follows: produce a schematic version of an organ based upon the case of an animal in which it has taken its most developed form (e.g. the torpedo ray's electric organs); operate topological deformations on it to demonstrate a continuity with other animals in which development of this organ may be retarded or distorted by the 'balancing of organs'; progressively reassemble different regions upon which this procedure has been carried out so as to gradually construct a map of the 'unified plan of composition', a speculative abstraction from which all animals can be derived (Cahn, *La Vie et l'œuvre*, 119). It is in this way that Geoffroy moves the model of biology away from arbitrary classification and toward a speculative morphology.

In a second and even more decisive stage, faced with cases where developed animals do not provide the resources to test his hypotheses, Geoffroy has recourse not only to palaeontology but to embryology and teratology (see Appel, *The Cuvier-Geoffroy Debate*, 125–30), both of which he 'advocated and practiced systematically for the first time' (ibid., 108). He can now think outside the time-funnel of actuality, seeking continuities that are invisible to poor Cuvier, reliant as he is on the present-being of speciated adults locked into an eternal present of compartments and branches. Geoffroy becomes a time-traveller. Not only does he see a fish's pectoral fin morph into the bones of a mammal's front limb and a fossilised saurian mutate into a crocodile, he travels along embryological lines of development that reveal homologies between the skull of a fish and that of a mammal foetus or between the sternum of a fish and that of an avian foetus; he confirms that whales do indeed have teeth, but only before they are born... comparative anatomy becomes ovology, in a decisive moment for the history of biological thought: as pronounced triumphantly later by egg-man Albert Dalcq (Deleuze's major source: A. Dalcq, *L'Œuf et son dynamisme organisateur* [Paris: Albin Michel, 1941]; see note 7, p53ff on this matter), from this point on 'whatever problem is raised by zoology, comparative anatomy, or palaeontology, it must, in the final analysis, be rethought in embryological terms' (cited in Cahn, *La Vie et l'œuvre*, 117). *21 November 1800: History of the Formation of the Egg*.

When considering form, first assume maximum plasticity, then turn to the deformed and the as-yet unformed. Plasm, egg, monster: this is the trinity that enabled Geoffroy to set an abstract and synthetic approach against Cuvier's allegiance to the 'school of facts' (Perrier, *Philosophy of Zoology*, 104), proposing the necessary speculative framework within which to distribute facts to maximum effect, and opening up a morpho-philosophical field that would prove decisive (via Goethe among others) in evolutionary biology and beyond.

While we do not seek to apply Geoffroy's biological thinking directly to the cuteness of the contemporary situation, its transcendental orientation is crucial when considering the relation between the virtualities of Cute and biological actuality. Accelerationism has always been a transcendental stance, and Geoffroy anticipates accelerationism's rejection of the structures of the present and its extrafactual assumption of plasticity, continuity, and mutation as a means to access the virtual past which constitutes the synthetic material of the future (regression=acceleration; the present is the brake), rather than judging the future (and therefore defending against it) by the standards of the present. Mapping the plane of composition and redistributing the catalogue of existing animals across its n-dimensional matrix is a prelude to the counteractualisation of the given, the production of new passages, and the actualisation of latent spaces (see Mackay, 'Hyperplastic Supernormal').

Now, while Geoffroy takes an abstract view, seeing passages between actual animals as necessary constructs without a care as to whether they are 'actually possible', to Cuvier these transformations and foldings are insufferable figments (the 'chain [...] of simultaneous and nuanced forms, which has reality only in the imagination' [Cuvier, cited in Appel, *The Cuvier-Geoffroy Debate*, 105]; 'Cuvier assumed that if the transformations were not *physically* conceivable—if one set of bones could not be topologically remolded into the other—then homologies were meaningless' [ibid., 140]), potentially deadly ('forced movements of a scope which would break any skeleton or tear ligaments' [Deleuze, *Difference and Repetition*, 215]— 'The very idea would frighten the imagination!', ibid., 151; *an adult would be torn apart by them...*), and no doubt 'against Nature'. Exasperated, like Sylvie, at these topo-illogical stories of animals getting 'squoze' and/or 'squeezeled', Cuvier exclaims '"I don't believe no crocodile ever walked along its own forehead", too much excited by the controversy to limit the number of his negatives' (Carroll, *Sylvie and Bruno*, 230–31). Cuvier sees only correlations between similarly functioning organs where Geoffroy sees 'connections, physical and mechanical relations, relations of position and transmission' (Jean Piveteau, quoted in Cahn, *La Vie et l'oeuvre*, 119). Since for him it is not morphology but physiology that is 'the essential part and the true aim of Zoology' (ibid., 31), he can only think of organs in terms of functions—which would surely break down during such unnatural passages!—whereas Geoffroy makes himself a body without organs. And one open to the great outdoors—his transformist insistence that 'ecological conditions have a great power to alter organized bodies' (Perrier, *Philosophy of Zoology*, 83), which Cuvier resists with what ultimately amounts to a finalism (*a confused kind of theism is hidden behind your insistence on the sovereignty of fact!*): all organs are perfectly suited to the needs of an animal designed and defined once and for all, in an eternally decreed present, and there is no call for any hypothesis of change or adaptation (Appel, *The Cuvier-Geoffroy Debate*, 137–8) or for the envisioning of a virtuality that would extend beyond the bounds of the actual.

Let us finally note that 'the fecundity of the idea of the unity of the plane of composition is revealed in striking fashion [...] particularly in [Saint-Hilaire's] studies on the comparative anatomy of the male and female sexual apparatuses' (as reported by Cuvier, cited in Cahn, *La Vie et l'œuvre*, 101). Between ostrich and cassowary, cock and hen, foreskin and bursa, ovaries and testicles, fallopian tubes and epididymis, uterine horns and vas deferens, uterus and seminal vesicles, clitoris and penis, vagina and foreskin, the visionary Geoffroy sees not the containing lines of Nature's forms, but a morphing array of involutions and eversions, infoldings and outpouchings, a calculus of virtual operations. Folding girls into boys is after all just a matter of 'relative sizes and inversions' (ibid., 102–103), dart-objects and wedges, bussies and girldicks, a continuum of reversible intertouchings (see note 60, p93). Geoffroy realignment surgery. 'Not just anyone can do this' (see note 58, p92)! *6 November 1800: Exploration of a Plan of Experiments to Arrive at the Proof of the Coexistence of the Sexes in the Germs of All Animals*: a 'crucial problem for psychoanalysis' indeed (see the 'translator's interface' to Alliez and Bonne, *Duchamp Looked At*, A281–84/B241–44). 'And how are we to join up these mysterious—no, I mean this mysterious opening?' (Carroll, *Sylvie and Bruno Concluded*, 101).

On the other hand (but these incongruent counterparts are beyond chirality...), as a formidable paragon of Royal Science—who stayed home at the 'centre of science' while Geoffroy took off on the transcendental trip to Egypt where the eccentric hero would develop his delirious Laplacian 'grand synthesis', a 'vast theory' of universal attraction and repulsion involving '"molecules" of caloric [...] pyramidal in form' alongside 'lavish plans' for the endian conversion of 'long eggs into short eggs' (Appel, *The Cuvier-Geoffroy Debate*, 72–3, 79, 77, 79, 65); which came first, the pyramid or the egg? (see p11)—the immovable Cuvier incarnates the alliance between finalism, functionalism, presentism, obsession with scientific fact as final arbiter of Reality, reactionary fear of unnatural speculation, and a gerontocratic conservatism that does not wish to hear about becomings.

Now, '[s]ome may well think [we] should refrain from reporting these facts in order not to offend persons in their mature years whose long experience has left them less receptive to seductive ideas...' (Geoffroy, cited in Perrier, *Philosophy of Zoology*, 100). '[A]nd yet, these alluring phantoms are the very driving force [...] responsible [...] for showing the route that will open new horizons' (ibid., 75). 'Anatomy was for a long time descriptive and particular, [but] nothing will stop it in its tendency to become general and philosophical' (Geoffroy, cited in Appel, *The Cuvier-Geoffroy Debate*, 139).

79.   Appel, *The Cuvier-Geoffroy Debate*, 105, 112.

80.   See T. Moynihan, *Spinal Catastrophism: A Secret History* (Falmouth: Urbanomic, 2020).

81.   Literary chonk Honoré de Balzac, who adored Cuvier, describing him in *La Peau du Chagrin* (1831) as an 'enchanter' and 'the greatest poet of our century', nonetheless turned to Geoffroy Saint-Hilaire (to whom he had dedicated *Père Goriot* following his meeting with the scientist in the spring of 1835) in the 1842 preface to *La Comédie humaine*, where the novelist salutes Geoffroy as 'he who triumphed over Cuvier', and ponders upon extending the idea of the 'Unity of Plan' to the 'social species' (see S. Collet, 'The Evolution of Social Species in Balzac's Comédie Humaine', in *Biological Time, Historical Time: Transfers and Transformations in 19th Century Literature* [*Faux Titre* 431] [Leiden: Brill, 2018], 241–57). In the 1867 novella *Guide-Âne a l'usage des animaux qui veulent parvenir aux honneurs* [*Beginn-asses Guide for Animals Who Want to Make it Big*], Balzac satirises the debate between Cuvier ('Cerceau') and Geoffroy, 'Prometheus of the natural sciences' and perpetrator of 'the massacre

of vertebrates and molluscs, of articulates and rays, from mammals to cirrhopods, from acephalans to crustaceans! No more Echinoderms, Acalepha or Infusoria! At last, you are breaking down all the partitions invented by Baron Cerceau!'.

A donkey narrator tells of how, with the connivance of a journalist who has painted him with stripes, his owner Adam Marmus becomes celebrated by *le tout Paris* as an intrepid naturalist who 'has brought back from the mountains of the Moon a Zebra whose peculiarities significantly disturb the fundamental ideas of zoology and prove right the illustrious philosopher who does not admit any difference in animal organization, and who proclaimed, to the applause of the learned men of Germany, the great principle of one and the same contexture for all animals'. Marmus's theory of 'instinctology' creates 'uproar' as 'animality is turned upside down'; Cerceau is eventually defeated by this audacious new theory which has proved that 'there was no longer any distinction to be made between Animals other than for the pleasure of collectors. Natural science had become a plaything! The oyster, the polyp, the coral, the lion, the zoophyte, microscopic animalcules, and man were all the same apparatus, simply modified by means of more or less elongated organs.' H. de Balzac in P.-J Stahl, *Scènes de la vie privée et publique des animaux* (Paris: J. Hetzel et Paulin, 1842), 183–208.

82.   Were the 'immense variety of animals and species of different shapes and functions' (E. Delacroix,
The Journal of Eugène Delacroix, tr. L. Norton [Ithaca,
NY: Cornell University Press, 1980], 55) among which
Geoffroy worked in the Museum d'Histoire Naturelle
reflected in the 'turpitudes' of 'an art where ground
carries away form' (É. Alliez with J.-C. Martin, *The
Brain-Eye: New Histories of Modern Painting*, tr. R.
Mackay [London and New York: Rowman and Littlefield, 2016], 77, 59)? Namely, in Delacroix's 'hallucino-
genic menagerie' [...] uniting plants with zebras' (ibid,
88): Delacroix who broke colour out of the line to flee
the formalisms of neoclassicism, Delacroix for whom
'there are lines that are monsters' (E. Delacroix, *Journal
(1822–1863)* [Paris: Plon, 1996], 89), and in whose
painting a lion's devouring of a horse becomes a tera-
tological metamorphosis, what Éric Alliez describes as
a 'massacre of painting' (Alliez, *The Brain-Eye*, chapter
2) to match the 'massacre of vertebrates and molluscs,
of articulates and rays, from mammals to cirrhopods,
from acephalans to crustaceans' that Balzac attributes to Geoffroy (see note 81, p105). Alliez sees in the
1854–6 *Lion Hunt*s an 'apparent unity of plane of composition of the multiple that gives free rein to the expression of mobile traits [...] to cross over the partitions between species [...] in a mutual exaltation in
which all embryonic forms are mixed' (Alliez, *The
Brain-Eye*, 89), beyond even the 'abomination' of
1827's *Death of Sardanapalus*. In great voyages—

Goethe's 'flight to Italy', Delacroix in Tangiers, Geoffroy in Egypt where (*semper aliquid novi*) he fomented the transcendental ambitions that would isolate him from his colleagues upon returning home, only to slowly work their way out of suppressed latency in his biological writings (Appel, *The Cuvier-Geoffroy Debate*, 81–82)—empirical dislocations open up transcendental perspectives. 'The voyage is intensive, it's true. But it does happen. For real' (J.-C. Goddard, *A Scabby Black Brazilian*, tr. T. Murphy with M.B. Kronic [Falmouth: Urbanomic, 2023], 44; Goddard's account of Lévi-Strauss's uneventful sojourn in Brazil [27–39] stands as a salutary counterexample). On the connection between Delacroix and Geoffroy see also A.A. Lang, 'Re-envisioning the Natural World in Eugène Delacroix's Lion Devouring a Horse', MA Thesis, Dept. of Art and Art History, University of Utah, 2016. More recently, see Japanese artist Satoshi Kawasaki's illustrations for a directly illustrative and appropriately humorous depiction of Geoffroyesque principles of anatomical origami, e.g. カメの甲羅はあばら骨 [*A Turtle's Shell is a Human's Ribs*] (Tokyo: SB Creative, 2019).

83.   Deleuze and Guattari, *A Thousand Plateaus*, 164.

84.   Ibid., 47.

85.   Deleuze, *Difference and Repetition*, 219, 118.

86.   Deleuze and Guattari, *A Thousand Plateaus*, 29. (See also Goddard, *A Scabby Black Brazilian*, 23–26.)

87.   'The question is fundamentally that of the body—the body they steal from us in order to fabricate opposable organisms. This body is stolen first from the girl: Stop behaving like that, you're not a little girl anymore, you're not a tomboy, etc. The girl's becoming is stolen first, in order to impose a history, or prehistory, upon her. The boy's turn comes next, but it is by using the girl as an example, by pointing to the girl as the object of his desire, that an opposed organism, a dominant history is fabricated for him too. The girl is the first victim, but she must also serve *as an example and a trap*. That is why, conversely, the reconstruction of the body as a Body without Organs, the anorganism of the body, is inseparable from a becoming-woman' (Deleuze and Guattari, *A Thousand Plateaus*, 276, emphasis ours).

88.   Ibid., 47.

89   Étienne Geoffroy Saint-Hilaire, cited in Appel, *The Cuvier-Geoffroy Debate*, 76.

90.   Deleuze and Guattari, *A Thousand Plateaus*, 276.

91.   'THE SIMULACRA IS STRUGGLING TO ESCAPE FROM THE PRISON WOMB [...] THE NEW IS STRUGGLING

TO BE BORN. BRING A JACKHAMMER AND SPLIT THE UMBILICAL CORD APART.' N.T.R. Watts, 'On the Concept of Moé', *Urbanomic Documents*, 2021, <https://www.urbanomic.com/document/moe/>, originally published in *Yonq* 8, <https://yonq.itch.io/eight>. This staggeringly brilliant, joyfully uncompromising accelerationist text played a crucial role in the hatching of cute/acc.

92.   Plant, 'Coming Across the Future', 45.

93.   Every stratum has its own egg (BwO). That is, below the organisational threshold of every body lies a field of tensions or differentiations which to some extent (to be determined experimentally) can be reconfigured to produce a new actuality. This is what we call the 'virtual body', the system of intensities that becomes overlaid with maps and codes, partitioned, subjected to systems of sensitisation and desensitisation.

The notion of the virtual here is not essentially linked to the digital or to being online. Beneath the body that has been constructed for you, there is a richer field of possibilities, and some of them might feel cuter. And none of this is to do with identity, representation, or resemblance. '[T]he actual, lived emotion of having breasts does not resemble breasts, it does not represent them, any more than a predestined zone in the egg resembles the organ that it is going to be stimulated to produce within itself. Nothing but bands of intensity, potentials, thresholds, and gradients' (Deleuze and Guattari, *Anti-Oedipus*, 19).

Socialisation trains bodies to register, sensitise, or develop some zones and not others according to inherited conventions, and rigging (see note 95 below) tends to reinforce that training (your bodily proprioception alters depending on what clothes you wear, for instance), shutting down the virtual body. See note 105, p125.

94.   Plant, 'Coming Across the Future', 46.

95.   The word 'rigging' retains an association with superficiality, appearance, and presentation, while reminding us that everything cosmetic is technological. In addition, the rigging of the ship is what enables you to hoist the sail, which is what enables you to traverse and be traversed (Gilles Grelet—see note 2, p50ff). Another understanding of the English word 'rigging' is manipulative: to make an event work out the way you want it to, to put things in place to produce what you want; here, the term suggests the practice of hyperstition. The term was chosen as the closest term to the French verb *appareiller*. As suggested by its proximity to both *apparaître* (to appear), *appareil* (apparatus or device, but also specifically the camera), and *apparat* (ceremonial), the words *appareil*, *appareiller*, and *appareillage* can designate both a technical

equipping, readying, or provisioning (to rig or fit out, accoutre, array, provision, equip) and a manner of appearing or augmenting appearance, covering a broad spectrum of preparations which may be either ceremonial, functional or both—from making up a face or dressing (as in the English *apparel*), to fitting with a prosthesis. The English *apparatus* has the same root and often translates *appareil*. Cute is unthinkable without rigging.

96.   A. Nguyen, 'Eternal Maidens: Kawaii Aesthetics and Otome Sensibility in Lolita Fashion', *East Asian Journal of Popular Culture* 2:1 (2016), 15–31: 17; M. Honda, 'The Genealogy of the Hirahira: Liminality and the Girl', in T. Aoyama and B. Hartley (eds.), *Girl Reading Girl in Japan* (New York: Routledge, 2010), 19–37; 'Albertine [...] flutters about, comes and goes, and draws from her lack of attachments a certain instability and unpredictable character that gives to her power of freedom.' J. Dubois, 'For Albertine', quoted in Tiqqun, *Raw Materials for a Theory of the Young-Girl*, tr. A. Reines (Los Angeles: Semiotext(e), 2001), 3.

97.   Deleuze and Guattari, *Anti-Oedipus*, 4.

98.   Grant, 'Black Ice', 132.

99.   Bottom up.

100.   The shōjo may be described as a subject position that deliberately repels female adulthood and its social and sexual constraints, while constructing or participating in a 'nostalgic' world. It may be rewarding to counterpose the shōjo with Tiqqun's conceptual persona of the 'Young-Girl' (see note 111, p126ff): while corresponding on a number of points, compared with Tiqqun's counsel of despair, thinking with the shōjo allows a little more space for her voice to be heard and sheds more light on the relation between actual historical young girls and the ungendered or post-gender imperative to girl.

    The modern concept of the shōjo coalesced during the Taisho period (1912–1924), which, in Japan as in the West, saw the initial emergence of an economic role for adolescence—the period of 'latency' between childhood and becoming a parent and/or member of the labour force. Rather than assigning their daughters to domestic work, as a marker of wealth, newly-affluent middle-class families began to send them to boarding schools, which became the seedbeds for a girl subculture. Shōjo, traditionally little more than a demographic category for those being disciplined for marriage, became an identity actively adopted by young females, and the newly extended period of adolescence began to generate its own dedicated cultural milieu, a 'special shōjo world' constructed by these girls as a positive bulwark against the 'natural' economic currents threatening to pull them from their 'latent' state into the reproductive economy (J.W. Treat, 'Yoshimoto Banana Writes Home: The Shōjo in Japanese Popular Culture', in J.W. Treat [ed.], *Contemporary Japan and Popular Culture*, [Honolulu: University of Hawai'i Press, 1996], 275–308: 280).

The post-war circuits of consumer capitalism boosted the ascendency of the shōjo, finding in her a figure ready-made to take on the role of pure consumer, or rather soliciting her to inhabit a subject-position that would make of her a living sign, a symbol of consumption, a figurehead to motivate fellow consumers. From this moment on, the shōjo moves from a marginal position toward ever greater visibility, until 'in whatever direction one turns, the barely (and thus ambiguously) pubescent woman is there both to promote products and purchase them, to excite the consumer and herself be thrilled by the flurry of goods and services that circulate like toys around her' (ibid., 280).

This instrumentality of the shōjo figure made room for the further differentiation and consolidation of the shōjo subject-position, that of a spectral subject existing 'off the production line', 'lacking any real referent in the "economy" of postmodern Japan' and 'relegated to pure play as pure sign' (ibid., 281).

As this 'unreality' was increasingly knowingly adopted by shōjo and reflected in cultural trends specific to them, but which soon spread to other sectors of society, its gendered associations began to loosen: 'young women (and the young men that increasingly resemble them) participate in a uniquely unproductive culture. They effectively signify sheer consumption, and as such cannot exist as wholly "real" in an economy otherwise committed to creating value, be it in terms of goods and services' (ibid., 281).

From the sixties through to the eighties cultural associations between shōjo and kawaii intensified. In early Japanese literature, the connotations of kawaii, literally 'blushing', were primarily supposedly female docile, adorable and 'pitiable' qualities. The concept later broadened to include infants and the 'charm exerted by their helplessness' (Shiokawa, 'Cute but Deadly', 95), with neo-Confucian features of 'female virtue' ('fragility, delicateness, sensitivity, prettiness') also becoming incorporated into its range of meanings (ibid., 95). But the emergence of the contemporary concept of kawaii cannot be properly understood outside of the history of manga, and this in turn ties it to the burgeoning of shōjo culture. '[T]he changing attitude to [kawaii] in Japan was in part engendered by the manga tradition in the post war period' (ibid., 97), and the shōjo world's attachment to kawaii was mediated by the emergence of gender-specific shōjo manga in accordance with the neo-Confucian idea of differentiated education for males and females (ibid., 99). Initially these 'girls comics' were written and drawn by men, and the women that appeared within their pages were endowed with traditionally kawaii features (dependency, helplessness, etc.). But during the sixties and seventies an influx of female artists transformed shōjo manga into a more autonomous form which rapidly developed its own traditions, forms, and conventions. It was during this period of manga art, for example, that increasingly large eyes began to appear (ibid., 101), along with characteristic shōjo clothing featuring frills, lace, extremely long hair, and all manner of accoutrements fulfilling the function of shōjo aesthetics such as the fuwafuwa and the hira-hira (see Nguyen, 'Eternal Maidens', 16–17); from the eighties onward, elements of this fictional garb would increasingly be adopted as actual fashion by kawaii girls, rigging for the girlstack:

> Objects create collectives of feeling, sensing and experiencing, bringing people together through shared affect. Aside from understanding girl as a discursive subject, a gender and an age position that moves in linear fashion towards the position of woman, girl as an affect comprises an embodied knowledge and experience that can be revisited and recalled. It may both circulate unconsciously and be self-consciously employed to engage in feeling girl (ibid., 17).

With the 'rapid evolution of long-form comics written by women' (94) and the peak-shifting of the kawaii moé-elements of their characters, kawaii was subjected to accelerated development, refinement, and differentiation, and a 'specific set of stylistic features and patterns' associated with it were gradually 'absorbed into the mainstream' (Shiokawa, 'Cute But Deadly', 94). The male-gaze kawaii stereotype of early shōjo manga was transmuted into 'the new type of women featured in action-oriented [*shōnen*] stories' (ibid., 94–95) for whom being kawaii did not necessarily stand in contradiction to being a warrior or a 'beautiful fighting girl' (ibid., 120; see T. Saitō, *Beautiful Fighting Girl*, tr. J. K. Vincent and D. Lawson [Minneapolis: University of Minnesota Press, 2001]). In this way, 'the phenomenal success of the comics medium as a source of public entertainment' drove the acceleration of the '"cute" revolution' in Japan (Shiokawa, 'Cute But Deadly', 97).

It has therefore been suggested that the shōjo world and the cunning appropriation of kawaii by its denizens (see S. Kinsella, 'Cuties in Japan', in L. Skov and B. Moeran [eds.], *Women, Media, and Consumption in Japan* [Oxford: Curzon Press, 1995], 220–54) constituted a 'delicate revolt' that provided a 'palatable camouflage' beneath which young Japanese girls culturally confronted and to some extent shifted gender roles (Shiokawa, 'Cute But Deadly', 121). At the same time, the phenomena of shōjo and kawaii have become a matter for moral concern and controversy within Japan: Are the '[c]ute "boys" and "girls" […] spending horrendous amounts of money on music, clothes and cute "things" in Harajuku and Aoyama' (Kinsella, 'Cuties in Japan', 247) simply infantilised and petulantly refusing adulthood, or do these aesthetics have some continuity with traditional Japanese culture? 'Individualistic consumption and the cute values of sensual abandon and play, which provided an apology for consumption, were accused of undermining Japanese tradition' (ibid.), with '[y]oung women, in particular [bearing] the brunt of the criticism of consumer culture throughout the 1980s and 90s':

> Cuties have been scapegoated. Their recent and highly conspicuous participation in decadent consumption activities, together with the older association of personal consumption involving interest in fashion and emotional abandon with femininity, has helped critics of modern culture to point the finger at women. Overworked salary men have been encouraged to see the source of their misery as the new generation of stroppy decadent young women, who selfishly do whatever they wish and make unreasonable demands on men. There is a general consensus that, today, men are hard done by and humiliated by manipulative, choosy, cute young women (ibid., 249).

If this complaint of the salaryman and scapegoating of the cutie reminds us of *Theory of the Young-Girl*, Kinsella also reminds us of a pertinent fact that is absent from Tiqqun's analysis: 'In fact, in the first half of the 1980s, young women worked more than at any time previously in the postwar period', something which of course was also 'interpreted as another act of willful selfishness on the part of women' (ibid., 249).

In any case, none of this has yet slowed the apparently unstoppable rise of shōjo (including in new guises such as *gyaru* and its various subgenres) or kawaii culture.

Addressing the increasing difficulty of gender-coding shōjo, Horikiri Naoto speculates upon the extent to which this might simply be because the position of the shōjo, now quasi-universal, is a 'new species': 'I wonder if we men shouldn't now think of ourselves as "shōjo", given our compulsory and excessive consumerism, a consumerism that in recent years afflicts us like sleepwalking. We are no longer the shabby and middle-aged teacher Humbert Humbert who chased Lolita's rear-end in his dreams. We all have become the forever-young Lolita herself. We are driven night and day to be relentless consumers.... The "shōjo", that new human species born of modern commodification, has today commodified everything and everyone' (quoted in J.W. Treat, 'Yoshimoto Banana's *Kitchen*, or the Cultural Logic of Japanese Consumerism', in L. Skov and B. Moeran [eds.], *Women Media and Consumption in Japan* [London and New York: Routledge, 2013], 274–98: 281; cf. 'All the old figures of patriarchal authority, from statesmen to bosses and cops, have become Young-Girlified', Tiqqun, *Theory of the Young-Girl*, 17).

Treat argues that, in this light, the translation of shōjo as 'young girl', suggesting on one hand childhood, on the other the inevitability of binary sexual differentiation, is unhelpful: 'one might well argue that shōjo constitute their own gender, neither male nor female but rather something importantly detached from the productive economy of hetero-sexual repro-duction' ('Yoshimoto Banana Writes Home', 282–83). Anthropologist Jennifer Robertson points out that '[l]iterally speaking, shōjo means a 'not-quite-female fe-male'. The depiction in manga and anime 'of both teenage men and women without key heterosexual difference' reflects the same nonproductivity in the sense that, regardless of gender, they and their most dedicated readers are incapable of producing value in the form of labour or children (i.e. new labourers), but are consigned to a 'self-referentiality that qualifies the sign of the shōjo and that of the shōjo-like shōnen subsumed beneath it' (quoted in ibid., 293–4).

In a present which 'allows the social order cre-ated of massive, large-scale images to exist as a pre-existent stratum' (Yoshimoto Takaaki, quoted in ibid., 296), the shōjo can therefore be understood as a 'topos of the neuter, neutral sign' (Mitsui Takuyaki and Washida Koyata, quoted in ibid., 301), 'a category of being more discursive than material, an adolescent space without substantive or fixed subjective content, a point in the commodity loop that exists only to con-sume'. If, as Eiji Ōtsuka writes, '[o]ur existence consists solely of the distribution and consumption of "things" brought us from elsewhere, "things" with which we play[, not] actually tangible, but […] only signs without any direct utility in life [...] signs without substance' (cf. 'all exchanges are now exchanges of dilatory appearance', Tiqqun, *Theory of the Young-Girl*, 17) then '[w]hat name are we to give this life of ours today? The name is "shōjo"' (quoted in Treat, 'Yoshimoto Banana Writes Home', 301).

What of shōjo sexuality? 'Shōjo implies heterosexual inexperience' as well as a 'homosexual experience' that is essentially autoerotic (Robertson, quoted in ibid., 56). The emotional life of the shōjo is essentially narcissistic in that it is self-referential, and self-referential as long as the shōjo is not employed productively in either sexual or capitalist economy (ibid., 280–83). This question of the sexuality of the 'in-between' shōjo is also bound up with kawaii: the shōjo is not a coquette, is not primarily interested in whatever sexual attraction her stylings may exert upon others; their dedication to 'the cute values of sensual abandon and play' is oriented toward the artificial and unproductive: 'the shōjo's own sexual energy, directed as it is towards stuffed animals, pink notebooks, strawberry crepes and Hello Kitty novelties, is an energy not yet deployable in the heterosexual economy of adult life', a self-sufficient desire like that of the otaku, a 'self-gratifying and chaste narcissism' (ibid., 293). For the shōjo, the cute exterior therefore is less like a gaudy mating display and more like the outward sign of the a certain jealous guarded and secret autonomy.

Similarly, if shōjo 'always had "cute" things around them' and 'adorned their personal belongings [...] with "cute" (and often "little") things' (Shiokawa, 'Cute But Deadly', 98), one cannot refer this to the 'domestic' without qualification. Treat notes that Yoshimoto Banana's novels, representative of a contemporary shōjo world, are infused with a certain nostalgia, but this is nostalgia for a 'home [which] is not where the nuclear family resides [...] but that kawaii world made up of cousins, boyfriends and favorite pets' (Treat, 'Yoshimoto Banana Writes Home', 295). It is through their world of cute objects that the shōjo doubles their incomplete 'accommodation with everyday life' with 'resistance to that same life through [...] longing for another sort of life, one that never actually "was" because no such life ever "is"' (ibid., 302).

It is therefore possible to strike a more careful balance between the fact that, as Tiqqun repeatedly remind us, shōjo consumption is surely also a factor in production for contemporary capitalism, and the fact that shōjo and kawaii can be seen as having carved out a form of 'unproductive' resistance which does not necessarily entail a Young-Girlish cynical abandon to the flows of exchange value, self-valorisation, and craven dependency on the commodities with which she surrounds herself, making her (us) a scapegoat to be blamed for 'prolonging the disaster with joy and insouciance' (Tiqqun, *Theory of the Young-Girl*, 87). Like the otaku, the shōjo unreasonably accelerates certain capitalist tendencies in ways that do not sit altogether comfortably with the humanist, familialist aspects of capitalist reterritorialisation. In the example of the novels of Yoshimoto Banana, Treat suggests, today the shōjo world continues to afford its devotees—of whatever gender and age—'the power to imagine themselves and their place as other than the constraints of everyday life might otherwise dictate' (Treat, 'Yoshimoto Banana Writes Home', 285).

101.   'For many young [Japanese] men, cute fashion represents freedom and an escape from the pressure of social expectations and regulations. Typically these young men both wear cute fashions, emulate cute behaviour themselves, and fetishize young women—either real girl friends or syrupy sweet little girl heroines depicted in lolita complex comic books for adolescent boys. [...] For their part, young women—even more than young men—desire to remain free, unmarried and young. Whilst a woman was still a shōjo outside the labour market, outside of the family she could enjoy the vacuous freedom of an outsider in society with no distinct obligations or role to play. But when she grew up and got married, the social role of a young woman was possibly more oppressive than that of a young company man. In her role as an unmarried woman, she was pushed to the margins of society, but was still able to work as an OL on a temporary contract in company offices, spend her money on herself and her friends,

and socialise in urban centres. Maturity and marriage threatened to separate her from these privileges, and very likely to shunt her off to a small apartment in a remote and unattractive suburb, with only her devotion to her children and their school books to occupy her.' Kinsella, 'Cuties in Japan', 244, 246. See also G. Ito, 'The Pleasure of Lines', in P.W. Galbraith (ed.), *The Moé Manifesto* (Tokyo: Tuttle, 2014), 163–69, 167–68.

102.   Deleuze, *Logic of Sense*, 12. Strange to see Félix Guattari, still perhaps too adult and weighed down by political and psychoanalytical neuroses to foresee its potential role in what he salutes as the 'becoming Japanese of our future childhoods', dismissing Japanese cuteness out of hand: 'do not confuse these becomings with capitalistic infantilism and its vibrating zones of collective hysteria, such as the syndrome of puerile cute culture (kawaii), the reading-drug of Manga comics, or the intrusiveness of sickly-sweet music'. Reporting here from Tokyo, 'the Eastern capital of Western capitalism', remarking that Western trends arrive on Japanese shores to only be stripped of the 'spirit of capitalism', and asking: 'Might Japanese capitalism be a mutation resulting from the monstrous crossing of animist powers [...] and the machinic powers of modernity [...]?', poor Guattari apparently fails to even consider whether this might be two-way traffic, whether these 'puerile', 'polluting' Japanese 'syndromes' might make their way back to the West.

F. Guattari, 'Tokyo, the Proud', in G. Genosko and J. Hetrick (eds.), *Machinic Eros: Writings on Japan* (Minneapolis: Univocal, 2015), 13–16: 14 [translation modified].

103.   On escape vs. escapology see B. Singleton, 'Maximum Jailbreak', in Avanessian and Mackay (eds.), *#accelerate*, 489–507.

104.   If you want to see cute acceleration—actual cyberpunk—look at twenty-first-century trans communities. From snapping selfies to distributing memes to inventing new genders to sharing lewds to relaying egg-cracking initiations to black-market hormones to the crowdsourcing of experimental self-medication data to GoFundMe surgeries (all in service of the moving target of just-rightness aka euphoria aka cuteness), on the third circuit of acutification (see note 155, p186ff) every body that enters the pipeline becomes lube for the pipeline.

The third circuit collectivises anomalous desire and wires it into the black nodes of the second circuit to make things happen, accreting novel machines with which to eggscavate the first circuit and 'change nature', with the retarded antimarkets of aboveground capitalism left to catch up if and when the state approves.

Don't bow to reality, hyperstitionalise yourself, crawl networks in order to circumvent institutional impossibility, collectivise the means of transformation, don't wait in line, don't tell others what to do, seize agency by making yourself a patient.

105.   'The body without organs is an egg'; 'The body without organs is like the cosmic egg' (Deleuze and Guattari, *Anti-Oedipus*, 19, 281). If every organisational stratum carries its own egg (see note 93, p109ff), it is also important to remark that The Egg (plane of consistency—On BwOs vs 'The' BwO/plane of consistency, see Deleuze and Guattari, *A Thousand Plateaus*, 157–58) goes all the way down. And technology—the realm of those hyperplasticising machines that 'rear up and stretch their pincers out in all directions at all the other strata' (ibid., 63)—is an egg-proxy, offering ever-increasing opportunities to traverse the strata. Technology represents 'an intermediate state between the two states of the abstract Machine—the state in which it remains enveloped in a corresponding stratum (ecumenon), and the state in which it develops in its own right on the destratified plane of consistency (planomenon). The abstract machine begins to unfold, to stand to full height, producing an illusion exceeding all strata' (ibid.). And it is characteristic of 'late' capitalism that the technological developments that extend this destratified plane are increasingly driven by desires incubated in the most 'superficial' strata.

106.   Deleuze, *Difference and Repetition*, 250.

107.   Deleuze and Guattari, *A Thousand Plateaus*, 276.

108.   Ibid., 276.

109.   Plant, 'Coming Across the Future', 463.

110.   Deleuze and Guattari, *A Thousand Plateaus*, 6.

111.   Tiqqun, *Theory of the Young-Girl*, 18. As unbearably oppressive as it is prescient, Tiqqun's *Theory of the Young-Girl* brings to a near-climax the aptitude of the Marxist Left for peevish stealth misogyny. Despite its many insights, it is a text haunted by phantoms of lost immediacy and innate value, fever-visions of contamination and the loss of 'the most precious and the most common [...] human productions' (88), tormented by the need for 'notion[s] of grandeur or prestige' (90), 'content and meaning' (118) to be solidly tethered to tradition or political determination rather than abandoned to the market. Full of barely-veiled contempt, seemingly pining for intimacy, tortured by uncertainty (flirting is hell) and the fear of being spurned (rejection is worse), it reads as one of the most insidiously poisonous tracts in the long history of masculine gerontocratic resentment. Whatever good intentions a reader may begin with, they cannot help ending up wondering about the zeal with which the Young-Girl is repeatedly and vehemently condemned, and speculating on the provenance of the authors' fervour for

stripping and exposing, showing her what she's really worth, demonstrating to the Young-Girl that she has no autonomy over herself or her body, that any sentiment of freedom, power, or joy she might experience is in fact the sensation of being continuously structurally raped, and that she brought it on herself.

It is a queasy admixture of resentment curdling into misogyny, political self-righteousness, and existential despair typical of the ageing comrade thumbing grumpily through an issue of *Cosmo* as he puffs on his pipe at the local bistro. One imagines his anger at how '*contemporary woman*' has frittered away the freedom for which his forerunners in the struggle so bravely fought (50), before his thoughts wander and he begins raking over past rejections...and then consoles himself with the thought that the women he sees in the pages of this magazine, and those who read it, are after all not *really* alive (unlike himself, still in touch with an *eigentlich* 'intimacy with the self' [54], capable of 'true EXPRESSION'—hence the wrinkles [27]). He quietly relishes his certainty that her 'maniacal effort of attaining, in her appearance, a definitive impermeability to time' (52) will surely fail, since either she will be 'acquired' and her commodity-aura will fall away to reveal that 'she's a twat and she stinks' (85, trans. modified), or she will grow old, 'decay' (23), 'decompose' (45), 'rot' (88, 122), becoming as 'hideous' (29), 'formless' (29) and 'protozoan' (26) as she always has in fact been. She'll see what's waiting for her once she's taken out of circulation, 'demonetized' (88). Her neurotic relationship to time (55) will sour, for (as he knows) youth is 'what is incessantly LOST' (52) and what's left is 'nothing but old age and death' (101)—indeed, underneath all that make-up, her 'face is that of death' (120). Perhaps he even indulges himself in little daydreams in which, for once, he is the mover and shaker, determining her fortunes in the 'marketplace of seduction' (128), the 'desire market' (102), hitting her where it really hurts ('*What an insult! Rejected by an old guy!* [...] Has her market value dropped?' [80]). If she'd given herself the chance to really get to know him, if 'relationships previously ruled by immediacy' hadn't been so totally 'mediat[ed] by the alienated social totality' (56), things would have been different! But in any case she's frigid (62), impossible to love (72), and he's pretty sure she gets sad when she goes home alone ('far from any gaze [...] she sobs and she sobs' [122]). In her prime she might fool herself, but he knows well enough that it's just a 'reprieve' (23): 'before her decay has become too obvious', she 'gets married' (24); when she 'arrives at the age limit of infantilism [...] she reproduces' (39). Finally, he convinces himself that she only has herself to blame if she ends up single—she's 'her own jailer' (54), a 'slave' (24, 56, 127), a 'prisoner' (34, 54); she didn't even give him an opening, she 'establishes a space of *power* insofar as this space is not, in the end, *a means* to approach her' (51). *She's just not worth it!* And that's final. But maybe he should try calling her again, because she would surely benefit from his helpful insights....

But we are falling prey to Tiqqun's sophisticated irony. The Young-Girl is not necessarily either young or a girl. 'Young-Girl is obviously not a gendered concept.' Obviously, '[i]t's not the theory of the Young-Girl that is the product of misogyny, but the Young-Girl herself' (Tiqqun, '1999 Introduction to the Text', *Raw Materials for a Theory of the Young-Girl* [with 1999 Introduction], <https://files.libcom.org/files/jeune-fille.pdf>)—*obviously!* And yet...one encounters significant difficulties in trying to extract the argument from its undertow of simmering resentment; it is in fact so difficult to unpick one from the other that a deeper affinity seems to be at work, and this is part of what makes the text so powerful yet challenging to respond to.

The brutally divisive and simplifying power of Tiqqun's rhetorical strategy is apparent from the outset of this text undoubtedly designed to 'divide one into two' in Maoist fashion. A strict binary is set up between the passive dupes who 'capitulate from the outset' and those rebels who, controlling and channelling their annihilatory hatred for the Young-Girl, embark dramatically upon a terribly daring 'criminal path' to 'undermine Empire's forces' (13), the forces of 'Evil' as 'distraction' (117). *But I was going into Tosche Station to pick up some power converters!*

As a riposte to this virile heroism, it is tempting to deliberately adopt the passive position, responding

to every page 'she's just like me fr fr', simply counter-
ing its sententious harrying by ironically inverting the
perspective and adopting it as a positive manifesto
(an approach admirably pursued by Alex Quicho in
'Everyone is a Girl Online', <https://www.wired.com/
story/girls-online-culture/>; a related strategy is
found in Andrea Long Chu's Females [London: Verso,
2019]). But '[t]he smile has never served as an argument' (40), and since the Young-Girl is a 'vision machine' which functions as a lens for each to 'show what
they're worth' (13), let's correct YG's pronoun to an impersonal 'it' and see if we can extract the argument
from the festering clods of (ironic!) misogyny.

 Women and youth represent those dimensions
of human life—in short, the domestic sphere, outside
of heterosexual reproduction and the labour market—
that historically had remained relatively free from the
grip of capitalist relations on account of their oblique
contribution to the sphere of production. By the same
token women and youths had, of course, been unpaid
for their role in social reproduction, remaining power-
less and without agency, the object rather than subject of fantasy, in so far as capitalism had not yet
reached the stage where it needed to draw upon them
in order to fuel its continual expansion. They therefore
represented a reservoir of potential for the disruption
of capitalist relations (Tiqqun quote 'Baudrillard-Tris-
sotin' on this point, 47). But when women and youth
finally became inscribed properly into the capitalist

socius, what ensued was not in fact emancipation but a 'myth of emancipation' (ibid.): rather than youths and women actually gaining power and agency (which, after all, would require a true revolution), Capital ended up profiting from the selling of the *spectacle* of emancipation to its supposed beneficiaries, while they became mere relays for the transmission of its ideology.

The admission of women and the young into capitalist circulation is therefore contemporaneous and in a sense synonymous with the era of the Spectacle. It is in this sense that Tiqqun claim that '[t]here is no metaphysical affinity between the figure of the Young-Girl and women or young people, only a historical one' (Tiqqun, '1999 Introduction'), and that YG itself is the product of misogyny—that of the inherent patriarchal structure of Capital, which, with the advent of the Spectacle, only becomes more subtilised. Tiqqun do acknowledge that there is a moment in which YG is in principle not a mere product of patriarchy—'It is altogether concretely that she has eluded those whose fantasies she populates in order to face and dominate them' (24), and is 'emancipated from the domestic sphere and from all sexual monopoly' (30)—but this moment is immediately superseded in the fashion of a master-slave dialectic, for YG's ultimate 'triumph originates in the failure of feminism' (8); 'masculine logic conquers women without them noticing' (15), so completely are they caught up in the signs and simulacra they disseminate in the service of Capital.

This all takes place in the wake of the First World War, a period which saw the beginning of the progressive colonisation by capital of everything that lay beyond the sphere of production, in a movement toward the 'final moment' of the 'socialisation' or *anthropomorphosis* of Capital (18) which would see the extinguishing of real human difference (including that of 'personality', 'character', 'ancestral distinction [...] every specificity of class or ethnicity' [17]) and its replacement by exchangeable pseudo-difference in the form of commodity categories. Capital reaches beyond the sphere of production to command the complete integration of subjects via consumption and the perpetual demand for self-valorisation and self-reification (by way of the marketisable desires and opinions of the THEY—the Heideggerian reference is unmistakeable). This process spells the extinction of the subject understood as the seat of real difference and 'intimacy with [one]self' (18) in favour of a pseudo-subject (YG) as mediator of exchange-value. With the extinction of all of the opacity to Capital once presented by the subject's real difference and self-reflexivity, YG-subject at last achieves total passivity, 'absolute transparency' (ibid.) to the exchangeable fluxes of capital.

At the very point when capitalism celebrates its integration of actual youths and women into capitalist-democratic societies in which every individual is 'empowered', then, YG is the perfect candidate to become an 'ideal regulator of the integration of the

citizen into Empire' (16, trans. modified). YG is the met-
onymic figurehead for the cutting edge of Capital's real
subsumption of all human life without remainder (11–
14), as well as its first historical model (via the abortive
emancipation and exemplary pacifying integration of
woman, body, and youth into capital via the sphere of
consumption). The role YG plays is by no means merely representational or illusory: YG is a machine-part, a
genuine 'factor of production [...] the consumer, the
producer, the consumer of producers, and the producer of consumers.' (65); it operates as a regulator, a 'new
figure of authority' (16) in the service of the market;
more powerful than any disciplinarian institution, a
kind of distributed soft-cop in an age where power
and authority have been made supple and molecular-
ised. Capitalism invents nothing, after all, and YG (abstract) simply parasitises the preexisting historical behaviours, attitudes, and appearances of the (empirical)
young girl, symbolically connected to all the high-
ly-valued sentiments, all of the elements of life that
had previously fallen outside of the scope of capital
subsumption and posed a problem to it. From these
remnants, it pieces together an irresistibly seductive
fantasy world which anyone (not just young girls) can
inhabit, a world that successfully commodifies all of
those formerly indigestible elements, and replicates
itself by memetic contagion, spreading until it is ines-
capable and penalising all dissidence. What follows is
the forgetting of any aspect of human relations

indigestible by total integration and real subsumption, and their replacement by ersatz simulacra (a 'forgetting of Being' no less, again with an unmistakeably Heideggerian flavour [33, trans. modified]).

It can be seen, then, that if the virtual YG is a model, actual YGs are tokens, in that every one is equivalent to every other ('Whatever, if not her then some other one...' [83, trans. modified]). The ubiquitous presence of these YG-clones induces 'the pulverization of everything that slowed the total mobilization of desire' (44), driving both the '*production* of merchandise' (ibid.) and the imprinting of 'a false and pathetic metaphysics' (33) upon social reality.

The great tension that *Young-Girl* is at pains to expose is that whereas each YG clone is apparently 'freed' by the absolute lightness of its complete submission and transparency to everything that flows through it, at the same time it is burdened (given its exemplarity as a template or universal model) with the entire weight of the malign social totality it pilots. A considerable weight to bear, since YG emerges in the historical stage of capital where actual physical exploitation of resources is becoming increasingly attenuated, and is therefore required to continually serve as 'proof and support of the limitless pursuit of the process of valorisation when the process of accumulation proves limited' (34).

Tiqqun's condemnation of the lightness with which YG experiences itself will therefore come down as heavily as this historical gravity demands. It is beyond exasperating that YG thinks it is doing something 'fun', refreshing, novel, liberated, interesting, or even that it should think (or think that it thinks) that it is *alive*. It is only a slave granted manumission on condition that it perform the role of social schema and disseminator of alienation, that it become a vacant 'carrier' (107, 116), a kind of chromosomal transport for Capital, vehicle for 'the entire reality of the Spectacle's abstract codes', a reproductive vessel (42): 'Everything she sees, she sees as and thus transforms into a commodity. It is in this sense that she also represents an advanced position in the infinite offensive of the Spectacle' (111).

The appearance of Albertine-like 'freedom of movement' (34) and lightness belies the fact that all of Young-Girl's activity (which is not really activity but passivity: Young-Girl 'does not play with appearances' [35], 'does not speak [...] [it] is spoken' [36], 'doesn't love' [57], 'does not possess attributes' [53], etc.) is in actuality afflicted by a deadweight dullness identical to that of the 'disillusioned yet dogged persistence of the tradwife' (30, translation modified), since YG is no less encumbered than she by the responsibility of slavishly reproducing a whole social order (a task that YG executes with 'the automatism of the shut-in' [34], being nothing but 'an attribute of [its] own *program*' [50]). The conclusion? 'The supposed liberation of women [now it seems it *is* about women...] did not

consist in their emancipation from the domestic
sphere, but rather in the total extension of the domestic into all of society' (43; cf. 27: 'In the final analysis,
the Young-Girl's ideal is *domestic*').

One may have one's suspicions as to why this
'total domestication' of the rugged, manly world of
production would provoke Old-Guy-Marxist's rage—
tfw you get home from the factory and your once-
sexy-and-chic girlfriend starts nagging you about cur-
tains—but according to him, it also apparently
constitutes YG's own 'suffering', which she (let's face
it, it's a she) will not admit to, but upon which he insists: 'The Young-Girl is optimistic, thrilled, positive,
happy, enthusiastic, joyful; in other words, *she suffers*
(45; see also 35, 38, 60, 76, 110, 125, 127, 129, and then,
most telling, 135: 'It is only in her *suffering* that the
Young-Girl is lovable'). The minor tragic notes that Old-
Guy allows to Young-Girl's life, not without a certain
grim satisfaction, stem from the implication that she
is trapped in domestic trivialities and lives in the shad-
ow of her degeneration into a mother or wife—hence
her fall back into the circuit of reproduction, her inevitable fate. That and her inability to live up to what is
truly human, a shortcoming of which she is obscurely
aware when pursued by her own inauthenticity in mo-
ments of lonely anguish.

They only hate on YG because she is a gaping,
trivial vacancy, an empty vessel, a hateful vehicle,
nothing, a suffering nothing, nothing but a brainless

deluded meat puppet who never does anything. But...
not a gendered concept, *obviously*.

*And yet...*apart from a more compact style, how
much distance is there *really* between Tiqqun's 'trash
theory' and the notorious Adolph McGroot's contemporaneous satirical paean to the Yorkshire Ripper's
services to the Radical Left:

[T]he inherently political character of Sutcliffe's gyne-
cidal fury will never be too forcefully insisted upon. [...]
[C]apitalism is female. And if capitalism is female, then
gynecide is the only politically revolutionary agenda left.

The rise of feminism in economically advanced
western liberal democracies after the upheavals of the
late sixties didn't just 'coincide' with the disintegration of
insurrectionary resistance to capitalism and the demise
of revolutionary socialism as a political force. It cut its
balls off, both literally and figuratively. With its privatisa-
tion of dissent, its valorisation of self-indulgent female
narcissism, and its domestication of the political—perfectly encapsulated in the slogan '*the personal is the political*', feminism emasculated revolutionary resistance to
consumer capitalism and initiated the ideological legiti-
misation of passivity and conformity that helped secure
the unquestioned reign of a free-market 'consensus' of
guilt-free consumption in western democracies.

Global capital is now in the process of secur-
ing its long-term bio-political investment and women—
probably because of some gluttonous physiological

predisposition to consumption—are the great incubators of that bio-political capital. Every female is at once a locus of consumption and a locus for the reproduction of consumption; both a consumer and the potential producer of future consumers. Capitalism reproduces itself both literally and figuratively through the human female. Thus, a total feminisation of the populace, irrespective of biological sexuation, presents the most efficient method of guaranteeing the perpetual acquiescence of a satisfied and perfectly submissive consumer workforce, busily refining their co-operative skills for the workplace while cultivating a compliant domesticity at home with their 'partner'.

'Femaleness' is no longer just a biological characteristic but a vigorously enforced sociological condition, an ideological imperative designed to maximise the population's potential for docile consumption. Domesticating the political, feminising the political or neutering the political all amount to the same thing: gradually eliminating the capacity for refusal. [...]

[I]f capitalism is female, misogyny is no longer a piece of personal pathology, it's a universal political imperative. Female capital is the enemy of mankind. It's not personal, it's political, cunt. (A. McGroot, 'All Hail the Blessed Sutcliffe', *Whorecull* 1 [Jan 2001].)

In the chokehold of Tiqqun's renewal of Sutcliffe's 'visionary urban hygiene project', a diagnosis all the more violent for its miserablism in which righteous anger against the dehumanising Spectacle becomes an alibi for the deliberate regurgitation of every misogynist trope in the book, there are a few sparse opportunities for movement: Tiqqun acknowledge the aspects of contagion and regression ('alienation by contagion' [23]; 'Everything that comes into contact with her is degraded into a Young-Girl' [70]), and even the accelerative aspect that results when 'Young-Girlist formatting becomes more widespread', competition hots up, and 'a qualitative jump becomes necessary; it becomes urgent to equip oneself with new and unheard-of attributes: One must move into some still-virgin space' (19). But this of course is still equivalent to mere capitulation, and therefore to nothing.

And then, the whole analysis is suspended by Tiqqun's insistence that they are addressing a 'critical transitional situation' in which the Young-Girl is already 'out of date' (20) and there is therefore some opportunity for leverage against YG's attempt to 'cover life with a varnish concealing its far-from-rosy reality' (31). There are however few indications as to what form this might take ('Assaults will be launched' [13]; *Better let him sleep?*).

In short, Old-McGroot sees Young-Girl as a piece of instrumentalised superstructure, a 'purely ideological creature' (66), little more than a mule for the trafficking of the Death Star Codex secreted in her rotting ass. A kind of alienated, calculative professional careerist-seductress, YG is either a malign pricktease obsessed with assessing her own 'seduction potential' but reluctant when it comes to actually putting out, or she is an entirely passive, indolent conduit for commodities. In either case, *she can't really be fucked*, and that's what makes him mad. *Either do me, or get a proper job* (he means it historically, not metaphysically), *but don't try to drag me into your repellent world of domesticity*.

As Old-Bearded-Prosecutor-Marx hammers away endlessly, piling charges one upon another, 'The Young-Girl did this, The Young-Girl did that', Young-Girl-Marx secretly dreams her dream of the rosy dawn that will succeed the 'critical transitional situation'. It seems like it will never end. But not a second, not a single sentence is spared to think about what YG *can* do, what it might mean to (*Hold tight and spit on us!*) enjoy—whether you hear it as *endure* or *enjouir* (Lyotard, *Libidinal Economy*, 112)—to inhabit and embrace the subject position that Old-Guy violently decries with a thousand spiteful condescending insults designed to shame, to elicit self-hatred, to make responsible, to make culpable. Little interest in why one might prefer 'to become a commodity, rather than passively suffer its tyranny' (75) and what that might produce; no interest in those who are 'taking things that are meant to be consumed and going beyond [...] lifting something made for consumption and embracing that distortion as rebellion against our forms' (Watts, 'On the Concept of Moé'); no curiosity about why 'becom[ing] a cartoon girl uncritical advocate of capital for participation, allying yourself with schizo-capital by becoming-anime [...] is probably the closest I've ever gotten to actually sensing libidinal currents' (Caroline Foley, Cute pre-Committee stage communication). Because she's dead to him, and that's how he likes her best.

112.   T. Morinaga, 'For Love or Money: A Lesson in Moé Economics', in P.W. Galbraith (ed.), *The Moé Manifesto*, 127–35: 133.

113.   Deleuze, *Logic of Sense*, 9. Cf. the thought-experiment with which Poincaré explains Riemannian geometry: 'Let us imagine a world populated only by beings with no depth and let us suppose that these "infinitely flat" animals are all in the same plane from which they cannot escape [...] What geometry will they be able to construct?' H. Poincaré, *Science and Hypothesis: The Complete Text*, tr. M. Frappier, A. Smith, and D.J. Stump (London and New York: Bloomsbury, 2018), 35.

114.   Saitō, *Beautiful Fighting Girl*, 87–89. The primal scene: 'Miyazaki Hayao dates his own beginnings as an animator to his seeing the 1958 Toei animation *Panda and the Magic Serpent* during his third year of high school. His feelings toward the heroine, which resembled romantic love, made this first experience

of anime a formative one. [...] To love an animated beautiful fighting girl: this is tantamount to finding sexuality in an animated work. [...] And the experience of this sexuality exerted an influence close to that of a trauma on one of the most important artists in the history of Japanese animation. This fact has another, more crucial significance, because it appears that animated beautiful girls have actually fostered a continuous repetition of the trauma. [...] A generation traumatized by anime creates its own works that repeat the wound. That wound is taken over and repeated by the next generation.'

115.   Ibid., 126.

116.   The mid-noughties cross-media blockbuster *Densha Otoko* (*Train Man*) (novel by Nakano Hitori, 2004; film version 2005, dir. Shôsuke Murakami), which tells the story of an introverted otaku who saves a woman on a train from being sexually harassed by a fellow passenger and consequently begins a relationship with her, renovated the image of otaku culture in Japanese public consciousness precisely by interpreting drawn sexuality in this way and then 'curing' it via assimilation into the regime of 'real', normative social relationships.

   The response from otaku themselves to this narrative's overwhelming popularity among mainstream audiences is telling: '[U]pon completing *Densha Otoko*

I was filled with absolute loathing [...]. To me, this manga represented everything wrong in society, and my feelings only grew stronger as I saw the praise it received online. [...] The "they lived happily ever after" ending was disgusting. The woman fell in love not with the man as who he was, but the contemporary image of what a Japanese man should be.' Parzival, 'Love is Dead, Long Live the Otaku', 4, 11; *Artificial Night Sky*, <https://artificialnightsky.neocities.org/honda-san/kimomen>.

Parzival (—is 2D love like courtly love? Is the otaku a knight? Both undertake an immobile voyage: the otaku asleep at the keyboard, the knight asleep on his mount—then departing suddenly at infinite speed like an arrow!) finds a precious ally in Honda Toru, whose 2005 book *Denpa Otoko* performs a polemical takedown of *Densha Otoko* on similar grounds, the critique beginning with Honda's substitution of '*denpa*' (electromagnetic waves) for the '*densha*' (train) of the original title. '*Denpa*' also carries figurative connotations of passivity (as if being controlled from afar by mysterious forces), social isolation, and paranoia. Once a pejorative for misfits, weirdos, and alienated individuals, the word has been reclaimed by Honda and others as a term of positive self-identification, as well as becoming an important aesthetic category in its own right. See Kenji the Enji, 'On Denpa', *On the Ones*, <https://ontheones.wordpress.com/2019/06/29/on-denpa-a-guest-article-by-kenji-the-engi/>. For a

1980s precursor to *Densha Otoko*'s redemption narrative see Tezuka Osamu's short anime *Run wa Kaze no Naka* (*Lunn Flies into the Wind*) (1983).

117.   'i forgot ppl are legit attracted to anime boys and i saw someone say "LOOK AT HIM. y'all need to appreciate him more😳" like girl...he's lines #girl ...hes lines changed my life.'

118.   '[B]ecause so many of us have our desires or relationships already mediated, the switch from "sexting with my human lover on another continent" and "sexting with a language model trained on a collective consciousness composed out of a million sexts it learnt from" is a smaller jump for your body than you'd expect. In both cases, you are getting turned on by a text or an image.' B. Konior, 'The Impersonal Within Us', *Chaosmotics*, <https://www.chaosmotics.com/en/featured/the-impersonal-within-us>.

119.   Demonic ingression can be tracked through co-incidence, and the arrival of 'moé' is no exception. A coinage born in the 1990s of an input recognition 'mal-function' on Japanese computers that conflated *moeru* (燃える, to burn [i.e. with desire]) with the much cuter *moeru* (萌える, to burst into bud), the term circulated on 2chan as slang for the affection one could feel for two-dimensional characters, before eventually spreading to the wider cultural sphere in the early

2000s where it would begin to lose some of its specificity—often being employed by non-otaku as a simple synonym for 'cute'.

   An emergent concept, sprouting from the shifting sands of realtime cultural production, moé does
not have a single stable definition. It nonetheless possesses various traits that display relative continuity
since its initiation and upon which most otaku will in-
sist: (1) Moé cannot be felt for three-dimensional beings. (2) Although its source is semiotic, it invariably
has a bodily dimension, manifesting as a physical response ('The little girl [...] knows that the more the
events traverse the entire, depthless extension, the
more they affect bodies...' [Deleuze, *Logic of Sense*,
12]). (3) It is inhuman, even when its object is anthro-
pomorphised, and this is part of its salutary power. (4)
It shares a large part of its affective field with cuteness (having evolved, on some accounts, directly out
of the consumption of shōjo manga [see note 100,
p114–15], the neotenous stylistic conventions of which
have become classic moé triggers).

   In addition, it is worth remarking that there is a
nontrivial relationship between moé and gender non-
conformity. See, for instance, H. Momoi, 'The Voice of
Moé Asks for Understanding: The Struggle against
Gender Norms', in Galbraith (ed.), *The Moé Manifesto*,
73–79; Ito, 'The Pleasure of Lines', in ibid., 163–69; P.W.
Galbraith, '*Moé*: Exploring Virtual Potential in Post-
Millennial Japan', *Electronic Journal of Contemporary*

Japanese Studies (October 2009), <http://www.japa-nesestudies.org.uk/articles/2009/Galbraith.html>; 'Akamatsu-sensei Talks "Moé"', *Matthew's Anime Blog*, 20 July 2005, <https://archives.4-ch.net/anime/kare-ha.pl/1122583157/>, and Watts, 'On the Concept of Moé'. Positive discussions of moé and nijikon have also found a place in the asexual and fictosexual communities, e.g. Anonymous, 'Why is anime and being attracted to fictional characters looked down upon?', *Asexuality.org*, <https://www.asexuality.org/en/top-ic/204455-why-is-anime-and-being-attracted-to-fic-tional-characters- looked-down-upon/>; NTU-Otastudy Group, 'Fictosexual Manifesto', <https://vocal.media/humans/fictosexual-manifesto>; and see V-M. Karhulahti and T. Välisalo, 'Fictosexuality, Fictoromance, and Fictophilia: A Qualitative Study of Love and Desire for Fictional Characters', *Frontiers in Psychology* 11 (January 2021): 6, 8.

From the point of view of cute/acc, moé is a material response to two-dimensional media that undoes semiotic/bodily and real/fictional dichotomies via the actualisation of hidden virtualities (tagged by moé-elements) embedded in both the future of digital media as an object of consumption, and the future of the consumer as a subject in transformation. To quote Parzifal (paraphrasing Honda Toru in 'Love is Dead, Long Live the Otaku', 20): 'Society is not ready for moé.'

120.   For Saitō, moé can neither be understood in terms of a disconnection from reality via retreat into an inner world, nor as a projection of (frustrated) internal desire. This is because the representational logic of manga and anime is culturally non-Western, which is to say it constructs an autonomous, collective, and exteriorised economy of desire that cannot be measured in terms of a reality/fiction hierarchy: 'In Japanese space the distinction between fiction and reality is not completely in effect. The distinction itself is in fact based on a Western idea. [...] In the Western space of popular culture [c]onstant and meticulous efforts are made [...] to prevent drawn images from attaining their own autonomous reality. In other words, drawn images are always kept in the position of being substitutes for objects that exist in reality.' While 'in Western space reality is always in the superior position, and the fictional space is not allowed to encroach on it', with various prohibitions being 'introduced to establish and maintain this superiority', in Japanese space, 'fiction itself is recognized as having its own autonomous reality'—'We do not enjoy fiction because it is a form of virtual reality. We enjoy it because of its status as another reality, one that demands a rearrangement of the subject' (Saitō, *Beautiful Fighting Girl*, 152, 156, 153, 162).

        Hence the strange indifference, self-sufficiency, and invincibility of 2D love. Its reality is just as material, social, and satisfying as the 'standard' reality (with its platitudinous mimetic logic) that the moé otaku or more recently in Chinese culture, the *zhixinglianren* ('2D lover'), has chosen to forego. In 'The Love Revolution is Here', Honda Toru emphasises the accelerating effect of a hypermediated, ever-densifying technological environment on the obsolescence of the old Platonic order: 'It may seem that moé is compensatory, but [...] it is often the other way around. People don't imagine a relationship with an anime character because they couldn't find a girlfriend, but rather they fell in love with a character in the first place. Any relationship with a human woman after that is compensatory. We have grown up in a media environment where it is possible to fall in love with manga and anime characters. Some people never stop feeling love for them' (125). Elsewhere, Honda quite rightly sees in this a Nietzschean operation. See T. Honda, 'I May Not be Popular but I Live On', *Frogkun*, <https://frogkun.com/2016/11/24/i-may-not-be-popular-but-i-live-on/> and Parzival's gloss on Honda's philosophy in 'Love is Dead, Long Live the Otaku', 17–18.

121.   Honda, 'The Love Revolution is Here', 118; Higashimura Hikaru, 'The Moé Studies Research Circle', in Galbraith (ed.), *The Moé Manifesto*, 126–43: 141.

122.   '[I]n capitalism, fiction is no longer merely representational but has invaded the Real to the point of constituting it.' M. Fisher, *Flatline Constructs: Gothic*

Materialism and Cybernetic Theory-Fiction (New York: Exmiliary Collective, 2018), 25–6.

123.   Parzival, 'Love is Dead, Long Live the Otaku', 20. The '2.5D' is Honda's coinage and names the interdimensional cultural productions and institutions —such as figurines, maid cafes, Comiket, Comicons, cosplay, and idol culture—that appear when the 2D world feeds back into the 3D world.

Meanwhile, *trompe l'oeil* fashion that inhabits an indeterminate space between two and three-dimensions has been making inroads since the late 2010s, from Gucci's 2016 2D-detailed cloak to Loewe's 2022 pixel capsule collection, via Jump From Paper's backpacks, MSCHF's cartoonish Big Red Boots, and ubiquitous bodyprint dresses. Couture, of course, consists entirely in transforming flat materials into three-dimensional objects whose allure will be otherwise potentiated when captured in the flat plane of a photograph. Along similar lines (planes), one of the selective pressures on the third circuit of acutification (see note 155, p186) is the incentive structure of attention-based platforms which reward users for reformatting themselves to maximum 2D effect (flatmaxxing: 'The Young-Girl resembles her photo', Tiqqun, *Theory of the Young-Girl*, 33).

124.   The Chinese phenomenon of *tangping* or 'lying flat', which has made itself synonymous with cute

memes of supine cats, mounts its protest against economic exploitation and social exhaustion in a fashion not dissimilar to the moé otaku's decathexis of three-dimensionality. While the *tangping zhuyizhe* ('tangpingist') advocates for a spartan, undemanding, and unambitious lifestyle, free of the pressures of property, marriage, and children, no matter how deplorable this might appear in the eyes of those still beholden to the propaganda of productivity and success (and indeed, tangping discourse has been subject to censorship by the Chinese state), the moé otaku chooses to opt out of 'credentialist' society with its dreary workaholic masculinity, its meek domestic femininity, its competition, judgementalism, and commodity-driven 'love capitalism', to embrace 2D love and lead a minimalist but happy existence on the margin: 'Otaku might come to be seen less as losers and more as models of happiness. Consuming what you need to be happy and not worrying about being the richest or most powerful might become the new standard'; 'As long as you manage to get by on the lowest living expenses possible, I believe you can find things to enjoy within yourself.' Morinaga Takuro, 'For Love or Money: A Lesson in Moé Economics', 135; Honda, 'I May Not be Popular but I Live On'.

   In both cases, it is flatness that opens the way for alienated outcasts 'at the bottom of society' (in the words of OG *tangping zhuyizhe* Luo Huazhong, quoted in E. Chen, 'Chinese Millennials Are "Chilling", and

Beijing Isn't Happy About It', *The New York Times*, <https://www.nytimes.com/2021/07/03/world/asia/china-slackers-tangping.html>), without wealth or cultural capital, to live a creative and fulfilling life, undertaking a great immobile voyage, constructing their own systems of values, and quietly defending themselves against the inertia of the bourgeois status quo.

The link between Deleuze's discussion of Bartleby's formula 'I would prefer not to'—which like the lover's 2D image annuls referentiality, eliminating the logic of copying in the same way that Saitō's 'Japanese space', enflamed with desire, deliriously calls new realities into being without them ever representing anything—and his invocation of a futuristic 'people-to-come', a people inaugurated by an experience of immanence, a people that stakes 'out a position on the path of absolute deterritorialization', a people notable for its 'exclusion from dominant systems' its 'excessiveness to any model', perhaps its 'failure to live up to any model', a 'dispossessed, [...] divergent and anomalous' people 'on the fringes of society', cannot be overlooked here. Not least because of the roots of the 'people-to-come' in Nietzsche's repudiation of Platonism and the prophecy of the 'strong of the future', the arrival of which, in the infamous accelerationist fragment, directly succeeds a great *flattening* [*Ausgleichung*]. G. Deleuze, 'Bartleby; Or, The Formula', in *Essays Critical and Clinical*, tr. D.W. Smith and M.A. Greco (London: Verso, 1998), 68–90; E. Berger,

'Synthetic Fabrication: The Myth of the Politics-to-Come (Part 0: Introduction)', *Vast Abrupt*, <https://vastabrupt.com/2018/01/12/synthetic-fabrication-pt0/>; J. Sholtz, *The Invention of a People: Heidegger and Deleuze on Art and the Political* (Edinburgh: Edinburgh University Press, 2015), 247–48; S. O'Sullivan, *Art Encounters Deleuze and Guattari* (Basingstoke: Palgrave Macmillan, 2006), 78; F. Nietzsche, *Sämtliche Werke: Kritische Studienausgabe im 15 Bänden*, ed. G. Colli and M. Montinari (Berlin: De Gruyter, 15 vols., 1988), vol. 12: *Nachgelassene Fragmente 1885–1889, 1. Teil*, 424–25.

125.   The susceptibility of the cues that trigger instinctual responses to exaptation by ersatz stand-ins grows apace with the increasing artificialisation of living environments, so that the entire bloody history of evolutionary selection responsible for programming us to seek out cuteness can be consummated in single abstract *puni plush* line. Human sexuality is no longer contained by the strictures of mere reproductive fitness.

In the nightcore OnlyFans *aidoru* baby-deer vocaloid furry rave of the dawning twenty-first century mediascape, it cannot help but overspill these bounds. The more synthetic our environments, the greater our access to latent spaces of virtual affect becomes, and the greater our access to latent spaces of virtual affect, the more synthetic our environments become—this is the supernormal-hyperplastic loop (see Mackay, 'Hyperplastic-Supernormal'). Karhulahti and Välisalo note the particular relationship between 2D love, supernormal stimuli, and the contemporary media environment in 'Fictosexuality, Fictoromance, and Fictophilia', 6–7, 8–9.

　　To those lost in melancholic nostalgia for the good old days when only Nature was natural and reality was the only Real, those who see in all of this nothing but incorrigible decadence, those who lack the fortitude and creativity of the moé otaku, whose experiments have opened up whole new terrains of desire—do not forget that it was this same feedback loop that coded the 'natural' drives in the first place (see note 152, p172ff). Animals evolve in adaptive responsiveness to their environments, so that their physiology, behaviour, and perception correlate with and correspond to changes in those environments. This is the basic programmability of nature, and nature is programmable because it is elastic—there is always a mutant surplus that ensures the contingency of every adaptation.

126.　Azuma, *Otaku*, 47, 52.

127.　The partial object is a psychoanalytic concept belonging to the theorisation of drives. While its development can be traced through Sigmund Freud, Melanie Klein, Karl Abraham, and Jacques Lacan (among others), it is the interpretation of partial objects in Deleuze and Guattari's *Anti-Oedipus*—where the abstraction of partial objects from some original totality or future unity, from 'the point of view of the whole, of global persons, and of complete objects', is at its fullest that becomes important for the cute/acc reading of moé—not least because such abstraction is what enables supernormality to function. 'We live today in the age of partial objects, bricks that have been shattered to bits, and leftovers. We no longer believe in the myth of the existence of fragments that, like pieces of an antique statue, are merely waiting for the last one to be turned up, so that they may all be glued back together to create a unity that is precisely the same as the original unity. We no longer believe in a primordial totality that once existed, or in a final totality that awaits us at some future date' (Deleuze and Guattari, *Anti-Oedipus*, 44, 42). Moreover, *Anti-Oedipus*'s break from the psychoanalytic tendency to think desire negatively in terms of lack and fulfilment undermines Azuma's (sometimes gloomy) understanding of database consumption as a form of 'animalisation' and supports Saitō's reading of otaku culture as non-representational and productive independently of his Lacanian premises. See *Anti-Oedipus*, especially, 42–50, 322–27; H. Azuma 'The Animalization of Otaku Culture', tr. Yuriko Furahata and M. Steinberg, *Mechademia* 2 (2007): 175–87, and Azuma, *Otaku*, 86–95.

128.   Contingency: 'The specific triggers of moé are all fads. [...] [W]hatever we might say about the things that these images of bishōjo share, none of them are essentially moé. They are just specific instances of things that triggered moé at one particular time' (M. Soda, 'The Philomoé Association: Discours de la moéthode', in Galbraith [ed.], *The Moé Manifesto*, 145–51: 148–49).

   Multipliers: N. Ito, 'Girl Drawing Girl: On Bishōjo Games', in Galbraith (ed.), *The Moé Manifesto*, 109–15: 114 (emphasis ours).

   Bodily: See, among countless other examples, Saitō, *Beautiful Fighting Girl*, 28–31; Ito Go: 'I find it somewhat dubious to simply define moé as desire. I feel it is closer to the feeling triggered by listening to techno or minimal music. When listening to rave, techno, and trance, there is a *bodily sensation*. At some point, what you hear is no longer the boring repetition of sound, but pleasurable music. Moé is similar to this. There is a moment when suddenly you understand and *feel* the pleasure of images and lines' ('The Pleasure of Lines', 163–64, emphasis ours). Azuma also likens moé to techno. Azuma, *Otaku*, 94.

129.   Azuma, *Otaku*, 42.

130.   Sauvagnargues, 'The Wasp and the Orchid', 180.

131.   Supernormal triggers and moé-elements share the characteristic of detachable abstraction—they are perceptual schemata separable from the processes or objects that produce them. They exist and operate independently of their original contexts and of any representational matrix. There is no meaningful narrative of survival, protection, and reproductive advantage urging the stickleback to attack a perceived interloper—an abstract swatch of red will do. And the redder the swatch, the more exuberant the attack. It is not a case of a convincing representation being mistaken for the real thing, the swatch of red simply makes something happen: '"partial object[s]" [...] are not descriptions but programs, "auto"-replicated by way of an operation passing across irreducible exteriority' (N. Land, 'Circuitries', in *Fanged Noumena*, 289-318: 295).

132.   In Azuma's work, the 'database' is a figure of postmodern anti-meaning. It displaces the 'grand narrative' system of the moderns—in which 'small narratives' are regulated by and can always be logically integrated back into an overarching grand narrative —with a two-level structure privileging the virtual configurability of elements rather than narrative coherence (a shift which takes place in otaku culture roughly around the mid-nineties with the release of *Neon Genesis Evangelion*). On the upper level of the database, configurations of 'fragmentary settings'—

intensities—take over the role of constituting the small narratives, while data is 'loaded' by producers and consumers (most often 'collectively and anonymously') into the featureless, inscribable memory bank that constitutes the lower level or the database proper (Azuma uses the term to refer to the dual level structure as a whole, as well as to the lower level on its own). The database is produced simultaneously alongside its consumption in the configurations of elements, it has no a priori content, and anything added to it immediately becomes part of the lexicon available for new configurations. Because every configuration of elements on the upper level of the database can be dissolved back into the lower level to be reconfigured, there is no meaningful distinction between 'original' configurations and 'derivative' configurations. See Azuma, *Otaku*, 25–63.

133.　'[E]very sext with a chatbot is an orgy with the unconscious database of desire which happens to be really cute.' Bogna Konior, Cute Committee Meeting, September 2023.

134.　Deleuze and Guattari, *A Thousand Plateaus*, 10.

135.　Guilt is an illusion grounded in identity instrumentalised to control revolutionary desire (see Deleuze and Guattari, *Anti-Oedipus*, 118, 120, 336, 350–51, and F. Nietzsche, *The Will to Power*, tr. W.

Kaufmann and R.J. Hollingdale [New York: Vintage, 1968], 268 [§485]; 281 [§518]; 338 [§635]). From identity we derive the subject and the object (the notion of subject conceived from outside), and this in turn licences belief in agency and intention (a subject that acts upon an object) which underwrites what we perceive as the law of cause and effect. If everything that occurs is caused by the act of some agent, then there is always someone or something to hold responsible. '[Responsibility] constitutes a crushing form of stratification. [...] [D]oes being responsible really put you on the side of the angels? We're so sedimented with years of responsibility, but this is merely a way to hang onto a sense of control, which itself is a part of the problem, not part of the solution' (Nick Land, paraphrased by C. Stivale, 'VirtFut3', *driftline.org* (1994), <http://www.driftline.org/cgi-bin/archive/archive_msg.cgi?file=spoon-archives/deleuze-guattari.archive/d-g_1994/deleuze_May.94&msgnum=31&start=1731&end=2001>). In short, the entire history of accusation, guilt, shame, resentment, and redemption can be traced back to identity. (Whereas 'Cute has no relation—its very makeup is alien—to responsibility. It is amoral [...].' May, *The Power of Cute*, 47.)

2D love is yet another form of desire crushed under the weight of a paranoid molar social caricature that operates to ridicule and dismiss it, 'protecting' others from potentially discovering their own lines of flight in it (and learning how to dismantle the shame they have been taught to feel) or from the pressure of wondering if their own unthinking participation in the regime of molar heterosexual reproductive relationships and the lifestyles they induce might not be the only way—that even if this strange kind of desire is not theirs, that maybe there are other kinds of desire, untapped and undiscovered, equally repressed and impossibilised, in which an escape route might be found. For it is not a specific content of desire that is important (this is how desire gets coopted by the police), rather what is important is to continue the work of critique which reveals the innocence of desire beneath the moralised social forms of investment that mark it as shameful or dysfunctional. A kind of work, an ordeal even, that is always accompanied by the difficult process of learning to undo inherited representations and stand up for desire itself. To ask, What are the molecular movements of desire here? And what if the molar investments were instead subordinated to molecular ones?

    'If desire is repressed, it is because every position of desire, no matter how small, is capable of calling into question the established order of a society' (Deleuze and Guattari, *Anti-Oedipus*, 118). Cuteness induces shamelessness, which is the beginning of transformation. And transformation is ordeal and labour (that of a second birth) since '[i]n the living being, the irreversibility of differentiation is followed by functional irreversibility' (G. Canguilhem, *Knowledge of Life*, tr. S. Geroulanos and D. Ginsburg [New York: Fordham University Press, 2008], 15)—but this irreversibility is itself a function of material and technological constraints whose material and technological disassembly only desire can initiate.

136.   Watts, 'On the Concept of Moé'.

137.   Saitō, *Beautiful Fighting Girl*, 31.

138.   'The trend is away from the real human body toward something cute. This is abstraction, but it is not unreal. The use of just a few lines enable us to imagine a certain three-dimensional entity, just like a mathematical model.' Ito, 'The Pleasure of Lines', *The Moé Manifesto*, 165.

   The secret exploited by every variety of maxxing is that reality is immanent to fiction. Here too, '[t]he ritual execution of successive graphic designs is effectual and active: it promotes the existence of the thing represented, "re-edits" it by having it pass through its successive stages of formation' (Griaule and Dieterlen, *The Pale Fox*, 99; see note 7, p62). Dogon database.

139.   'Dismemberment: countermemory. A new generation has forgotten what its organs were supposed to be doing for their sense of self or the reproduction of the species, and have learned instead to let their

bodies learn what they can do without preprogramming desire [...]. This is only the beginning of a process which abandons the model of a unified and centralized organism, "the organic body, organized with survival as its goal", in favor of a diagram of fluid sex.'; 'She did not, after all, have a single sex, a sex which belonged to something called herself. Her body had not simply been excluded from orthodox conceptions of being human: It had refused to go along with man's definitions of organic life.' S. Plant, *Zeros and Ones: Digital Women and the New Technoculture* (New York: Doubleday, 1997), 203, 206.

140.   Watts, 'On the Concept of Moé'.

141.   Plant, 'Coming Across the Future', 45.

142.   M. Foucault, 'Introduction', *Herculine Barbin: Being the Recently Discovered Memoirs of a Nineteenth-Century French Hermaphrodite*, tr. R. McDougall (New York: Vintage, 2010), x.

143.   A metaphysical error (in the terms of Kantian critical philosophy) consists in the collapsing of the process of transcendental production of objects onto a given object, as if it could be the source of that process. In Deleuze and Guattari's materialisation of Kantian critique, this becomes akin to collapsing the virtual onto the actual.

The principal methodological decision of this book is to regard Cute as a virtual Idea or problem which humanity has stumbled upon and which it is gradually feeling out, but which is irreducible to what humans might make of it at any given moment, refractory to the objects that might be produced in the wake of their fumbling relations with it.

More precisely, the 'Cute process' is the interference pattern between the human sensorium and some Thing (Cute 'itself') that is complex, consistent, and attractive, and which is undoing us to the extent that we refine our access to it. The products of this process are residual and of anecdotal interest. We hypothesise that something is happening, and in so far as it is an event, it can only be tracked by transversally moving between the disciplinary categories under which objects are ranged. It is remarkable the extent to which humans resist the thought that something might be happening; one way in which they do so is by committing (to) metaphysical errors.

Understanding metaphysical error is the key to understanding why the egg is regressive, but not in a temporal or historical sense: 'Time no more comes out of the past than it comes out of the future. Time comes out of the transcendental, which is not in time [...]. As soon as you try to think of time as being in time, you're doing metaphysics; as soon as you stop thinking of time as being something in time, you know it has not come out of the past any more than it comes out of the future. It comes transcendentally into the actual. It's the actualisation of the virtual, it's not something that comes out of the past' (Nick Land, unpublished interview with G. Aldous, 2017).

144.   Harris, *Cute, Quaint, Hungry and Romantic*, xv. Uniquely among 'critical' literature on cuteness, Harris's book combines rigorous Adornian critique with a palpable sensory joy; in his afterword to the book the author reflects upon his own ambivalent role as both 'scold' and helpless cutie.

145.   '[C]hildlike consumer behavior, namely, stimulus seeking, reality conflict, escapism, and control of aggression.' M.A. Oliver, 'Consumer Neoteny: An Evolutionary Perspective on Childlike Behavior in Consumer Society', *Evolutionary Psychology* (2016), 1–11: 1.

146.   'If such soulless insentience is any indication, cuteness is the most scrutable and externalised of aesthetics in that it creates a world of stationary objects and tempting exteriors that deliver themselves up to us, putting themselves at our disposal and allowing themselves to be apprehended entirely through the senses.' Harris, *Cute, Quaint, Hungry and Romantic*, 8–9.

147.   'Putting an end to the process or prolonging it indefinitely—which, strictly speaking, is tantamount

to ending it abruptly and prematurely—is what creates the artificial schizophrenic found in mental institutions: a limp rag forced into autistic behavior, produced as an entirely separate and independent entity.'
Deleuze and Guattari, *Anti-Oedipus*, 5.

148.   There is barely a pause between Lorenz's definition of the Kindchenschema and his acknowledge-
ment that the market cycles of the 'representational
industry' (Lorenz, *Studies*, vol. 2, 160) directly take up
the baton of acutification from the first circuit of abstractive cyberpositive feedback which had 'naturally'
honed the 'releasers, together with the responding
receptor correlates' that differentiated cuteness (ibid.,
154).

    Directly after introducing the Kindchenschema,
Lorenz writes that 'the releasing characters [*Merkmale*] of the schema are present in exaggerated form
in 'trash art' in the manner of 'superoptimal [i.e. super-
normal] dummies' (ibid., 159–60, translation modified).
Thus, 'inauthentic [*unechten*] creations generally described as "trash [*Schund*]", which are not dictated by
the taste of an artist but by the requirements of the
receptive public, as is the case with fashion designs,
cheap novels and cheaply made films', are cultural analogs to ethological experiments in supernormal stimuli, which emerge spontaneously from market dynam-
ics: 'Just as in the case of the doll industry, the
industries concerned carry out thoroughgoing dummy

experiments on a very broad basis with their public, since quite obviously the greatest financial success accrues to the producer whose product exhibits the greatest elicitatory effect' (ibid., 154; on this point see also Mackay, 'Hyperplastic Supernormal').

Lorenz points out that this second circuit of acutification continues the abstractive trend characteristic of releaser sign-stimuli (see note 153, p176–80), including 'clear-cut abstraction of the form and relationship characters to which the innate releasing mechanism responds', 'extreme simplifications', and 'the registration of simplified "abstract" proportional characters down to arithmetical detail' (ibid., 159).

One might profitably compare Lorenz's impartially proto-cybernetic take on the escalation of *Schund-kunst* with the dotty jottings of that most sophisticated of moaners 'Hippo King Archibald', whose analysis of the culture industry and the '*Stigma des Unechten*' sees in such trash no escalation but only inane repetition and the satisfaction of regressive desires for the recognisable and indifferent. According to him, absent the tension of a critical posture, this resistanceless stasis spells the very extinction of discriminative perception (*Jitterbugs ain't cute!*).

John Morreall repeats the complaint verbatim, specifically with reference to cuteness: 'Cuteness is unimportant [...]. As far as traditional art and aesthetics are concerned [...] cuteness is a second-class aesthetic property' (J. Morreall, 'Cuteness', *British Journal of Aesthetics* 31:1 [January 1991]: 39–47: 39); '[C]uteness has not been important in the high traditions of Western art because it is an unsubtle property, and unsubtle properties have usually been treated as inferior aesthetic properties' (ibid., 46); 'Cuteness requires no taste or aesthetic education to discern. That is why, of course, it is so common in Kitsch' and 'is objectionable in the arts' (ibid.). Cute 'can aim for only a passive response […] to portray a cute child in a painting, for example, is not by itself aesthetically objectionable, but to do so by painting the child's eyes four times the size of real eyes, with three-ounce tears in their corners, is objectionable. For it hits viewers over the head with its message; it tells them just how to react to the painting and so leaves them with no cognitive steps to go through', whereas 'aesthetic value is proportional to the effort needed to process the work cognitively' (J. Morreall and J. Loy, 'Kitsch and Aesthetic Education', *The Journal of Aesthetic Education* 23:4 [1989], 63–73: 68). When effective change can only come from self-possessed cognitive agency, when the vanishing of distance between subject and commodity is equivalent to 'identification with the aggressor', going with what you like cannot possibly produce differentiation, abstraction, or acceleration, only more misery and abyssal self-deception.

149. Although the sociobiological and evolutionary-psychological approaches may certainly be open

to criticism on the basis of the political uses that have been and are being made of them, objections can be more solidly based on methodological and conceptual problems.

There is no proof for the direct natural selection for specific behavioural traits. The very idea is based on a series of misunderstandings of the genetic theory of natural selection. The definition of the gene (unit of evolution) is far from settled, and gene-phenotype correspondence is not one-to-one. Selection is a matter not of optimal but of evolutionarily stable strategies (ESS). The question of whether an evolutionary strategy becomes stable depends upon its effects across a population, in competition with other strategies; an ESS is one that, all other things being equal, becomes immune to destabilisation by another strategy if a majority of the population adopts it—which is not the same thing as the optimum outcome for any one individual (inclusive fitness) or even kin group (kin selection). Proposing a story based on why a given behavioural trait is optimal for an individual or a species and therefore 'must be genetic' is therefore a mistaken endeavour on several levels. For the basics on all of this, see R. Dawkins, *The Selfish Gene: 40th Anniversary Edition* (Oxford: Oxford University Press, 2016), and more specifically R. Dawkins, 'Good Strategy or Evolutionarily Stable Strategy?', in G.W. Barlow and J. Silverberg (eds.), *Sociobiology: Beyond Nature/Nurture* (London: Routledge, 1980), 331–69.

As Stephen Jay Gould argues in the same valuable collection, the reliance of such '[a]daptive storytelling' on mere '[c]onsistency with natural selection' as sole criteria is liable to lead to '[s]peculative storytelling', producing fables which may wield 'political clout' but are entirely 'unsupported' by the scientific theoretical edifice to which they appeal ('Sociobiology and the Theory of Natural Selection', in ibid., 257–72, emphasis ours).

There are other good reasons to reject genetic determinism in relation to behaviour. As E.O. Wilson suggests, genetic inheritance can be said to supply at most a 'developmental topography' for human behaviour, with each individual case tending to fall into the various attractor basins or channels of the landscape it sculpts, *subject to multiple other forces* (environmental, developmental, cultural, etc.) that may nudge it out of the preexisting channels or even, over time, carve out new ones ('A Consideration of the Genetic Foundation of Human Social Behaviour', in ibid., 295–304). We can attribute to evolution only a possibility space—neither a prescriptive set of pathways nor an entirely saturated field of possibilities: 'it is well known to students of evolution that all of the general qualities of human social behaviour taken together occupy only a tiny envelope in the space of the realized social behaviours'. The path between gene and phenotype is culturally, politically, historically, geographically, climatically (etc.) mediated. This only becomes more

obvious as we realise that, for instance, twenti-
eth-century gender performance was a historical ar-
tefact designed to ensure smooth running of a particular social machine. At the point where it begins to
fall apart (which is where we are), causal pathways previously thought to be solidly deterministic reveal their
complexity and transversality.

Along these lines, E.K. Adkins writes that the
'considerable plasticity of sex-related behavior' is itself
'a highly adaptive product of our evolution, for it allows
each culture to arrive at a set of sex roles uniquely
suited to its particular ecological demands without
having to "wait" thousands of years for genetic changes to provide them' ('Genes, Hormones, Sex and Gender', in ibid., 385–415: 405).

Deleuze approaches the question philosophi-
cally in his introduction to *Instincts and Institutions*,
pointing out that individual experience presupposes
either a species milieu in which instincts allow the satisfaction of needs and tendencies via automatic trop-
isms toward certain external stimuli (instinct), or an
artificially constructed milieu in which an organised
system of artificially instituted means make possible
the satisfaction of needs and tendencies in other ways
(institution). An institution constitutes a positive model of action, unlike a law, which is a restriction upon
action, and different social systems maintain a different balance between laws and institutions. A biological tendency or need may indeed be satisfied by an

institution, but can never serve to *explain* the existence of *that particular* institution, since the institution neither triggers nor determines the tendency, and there are multiple other ways of satisfying it. A tendency or need is thus satisfied only obliquely or indirectly by an institution (at the same time being 'constrained or hindered, and transformed, sublimated'), so we cannot simply say that the institution is useful (or 'adaptive') without asking 'Useful to who?' In other words, there are always other factors involved in determining which institution emerges within a given society to satisfy a given drive or need—factors that cannot be explained either by the tendency itself or in terms of utility. The problem common to instinct and institution is that of the synthesis between the tendency and the object that satisfies it (G. Deleuze, 'Introduction', in *Instincts and Institutions* [Paris: Hachette, 1953], viii–xi).

In a highly artificialised environment furnished with an abundance of resources—that is, once 'man has been driven out of the paradise in which he could trust his instincts' (Lorenz) and response patterns have been effectively deranged by the technological redistribution of releasing stimuli—it is 'fallacious to assume that each behaviour exists because it guarantees an optimal likelihood of individual survival, or even because it confers a relative immediate advantage of one population over and against another' (A.L. Caplan, 'A Critical Examination of Current Sociobiological Theory: Adequacy and Implications', in Barlow and Silverberg [eds.], *Sociobiology: Beyond Nature/ Nurture*, 97–114: 110). In general, the fact that we can tell ourselves a story about why something is 'adaptive' doesn't mean that it is genetic. The circuit of cultural evolution produces mutation, innovation, development, transmission, and stabilisation by other means, operates at a different speed, according to different fitness criteria, and in a Lamarckian manner; it is also more diffuse, operating via rhizomes, with multiple crossovers, convergences, or anastomoses, not just branchings. See note 155, p186ff on the three circuits and note 152, p172ff on evolution.

150.   From one point of view, erring is simply what evolution does, and this errancy suggests neither a dead end nor an empty space, but a terra incognita, boasting an entire variegated landscape of untapped virtual affect. What from the perspective of an evolutionary psychologist constitutes a mating error, for the consumers of manga and anime culture becomes a productive process in which there are no preconstituted subjects to be led astray, just a concatenation of partial objects and drives, configurations of sensations—textures, intensities, aesthetics, and vibes.

  From another point of view, the category of error is simply not applicable to evolutionary processes, since it implies a well-defined aim, but evolution has no such telos. What evolution does is *variation*, and it is because of this intrinsic and functional variability

—errancy in the first sense, that of wandering—that evolutionary forms, robust in the face of environmental variations, have managed to crawl into every last ickle crevice of self-sustenance on the planet.

151.   E.g. A.B. Barron and B. Hare, 'Prosociality and a Sociosexual Hypothesis for the Evolution of Same-Sex Attraction in Humans', *Frontiers in Psychology* 10 (2020): Article 2955.

152.   Such 'panglossian panselectionism' aside (Caplan, 'A Critical Examination', 108), even before Tinbergen gets his paintbrush out, the question of the evolutionary basis of Cute is something of a gull-and-egg question, with the line between nature and culture blurring as we approach. The account recited chapter-and-verse across innumerable thinkpieces is that the involuntary human response to cuteness is a successful evolutionary strategy because it fixes attention upon the visual stimulus presented by human infant faces. But which came first, infant cuteness or adult receptiveness to it?

    This question is the basis of a philosophical disputation with a somewhat Carrollian flavour over cuteness as an 'aesthetic category' (Morreall, 'Cuteness'; J.T. Sanders, 'On "Cuteness"', *The British Journal of Aesthetics* 32:2 [April 1992], 162–65; J. Morreall, 'The Contingency of Cuteness: A Reply to Sanders', *The British Journal of Aesthetics* 33:3 [July 1993]: 283–85).

Morreall's interest lies in disqualifying cultures of cuteness from the respectable arena of aesthetic education (see note 148, p165–66; Morreall and Loy, 'Kitsch and Aesthetic Education') along with other 'unsubtle' properties with 'only functional status [...] which get some biological job done' (Morreall, 'The Contingency of Cuteness', 284) and to which one responds not 'as an aesthete' but as 'a limbic system wired to a body [...] in an unthinking, automatic way' (Morreall, 'Cuteness', 46, 47). Citing Lorenz, he sets out the familiar argument that 'at a certain stage in evolution, young mammals developed distinctively babyish features which served as "releasing stimuli" for affectionate behaviour from adults. These features had survival value and were passed on to succeeding generations' (Morreall, 'The Contingency of Cuteness', 283).

Sanders objects that the 'features that get infants noticed' (ibid., 41) i.e. the Kindchenschema traits, cannot possibly have emerged via natural selection because they were 'attractive to adult members of our ancestor species independently of the fact that infants have them' (Sanders, 'On "Cuteness"', 162)—as if cuteness were some 'fortuitous [...] quality' (ibid., 164) to which adults were secretly attuned and whose emergence they had been eagerly awaiting while grudgingly caring for generations of uncute offspring. Since adult attention to conspecific infants is an existential condition for any species in which the young require care, 'cute' cannot refer to particular features that are the product of some contingent evolutionary event, but must just be a synonym for whatever infants happen to look like—'Babies are cute' is (either logically or biologically) an analytic rather than a synthetic proposition, and inversely, 'it cannot be that cuteness, in itself, has evolutionary value [...] because ancestors of ours could not, in any interesting sense, have been uncute' (ibid.) on pain of extinction (i.e. the infants of a species can only 'be uncute' in the sense that, like insects for instance, they do not require parental attention at all).

Morreall's reasonable rejoinder is that cuteness is 'neither a logical nor a biological necessity'. There are likely extraneous reasons for the prior existence of Kindchenschema traits, there undoubtedly were and are other motivations for caregiving besides cuteness, and cuteness involves a subset of infant features rather than being synonymous with all of them (Morreall, 'The Contingency of Cuteness', 285). Cuteness is indeed a contingent event involving a particular set of visual cues *as well as being* tied inextricably to biological instinct.

However, it seems no less reasonable for Sanders to say that 'elicitation of nurturing' is a weak condition for cuteness to emerge as a selective trait, and this points to the fact that Morreall's attempt to naturalistically deflate cuteness is afflicted by oversimplifications and oversights.

Phenotypes don't appear overnight. Genetics operates in terms of populations and frequencies. There are not only adaptations but also 'exaptations', involving the conscription of existing vestigial features for a new function. Supposing a base level of bonding between parent and child necessary for the perpetuation of the species, even if Kindchenschema traits were generally present in a population and already served as one among many stimuli for caregiving, a certain proportion of individuals could carry mutated or reassorted genes that expressed phenotypically as especially pronounced cuteness and elicited exaggerated behaviour on the part of parents. By attracting more parental attention, they might prove statistically more successful in passing on these genes, leading to the accentuation of these more pronounced traits in the population and their gradual accumulation over generations. An extremely basic differential responsiveness to infantile features (and incidentally, contra Morreall, even insects respond differentially to larval stages of their conspecifics) could then give rise to a runaway process of heterochrony which sees those features becoming increasingly exaggerated, perhaps plateauing as an evolutionarily stable strategy.

In this way, cuteness would become evolutionarily significant by progressively differentiating itself from 'whatever infants happen to look like', developing into a set of heightened cues that ceased to be purely functional and became in a sense *conventional* (as conventional as the formalised tournaments Lorenz describes in *On Aggression*). Indeed, it is this kind of adhesion to the instinctive *and* its abstraction into a set of conventional aesthetic qualities that seems characteristic of the enigma of cuteness.

Involuntary response to cuteness certainly belongs to the domain of instinct, i.e. that of phylogenetically inherited rather than learned response, following Lorenz's refined conception of instinct which superseded the early twentieth century concept of 'species-specific drive activity' (Lorenz, *Studies*, vol. 1, xvii) which Oskar Heinroth developed through his experiments with birds with a view to distinguishing innate species-specific actions from acquired behaviours.

Lorenz sought to counteract 'the neglect of the presence of innate species-specific action and response patterns in human beings' (ibid., vol. 2, 116), insisting that 'the behaviour not only of animals, but of human beings as well, is to a large extent determined by nervous mechanisms evolved in the phylogeny of the species' (ibid., vol. 1, xii), that is, by '[i]nstinctive behaviour patterns reliant on 'inherited' not 'individually acquired pathways' (ibid., vol. 1, 5). What Lorenz terms *innate releasing mechanisms* (a concept modelled on von Uexküll's *Merkmale* and *Wirkmale*) are advantageous for survival because they 'permit the organism to respond in an appropriate manner, without previous experience of any kind, to the occurrence of specific, biologically relevant stimulus situations' *as if* 'the animal innately possesses "knowledge" of specific response-eliciting objects' (ibid., vol. 2, 136).

Note the '*as if*': Lorenz is at pains to distinguish his concept from the notion of a 'species-specific memory picture' (Jung) and the contemporary theme of Gestalt perception (Wertheimer), precisely because 'the innate releasing mechanism [...] does not respond to the overall total or even a large proportion of the stimuli accompanying a certain relevant situation. Instead, the mechanism selects relatively few of the great number of stimuli and permits these to act as a "key to the response"' (ibid., vol. 2, 136–37; on this point see also Mackay, 'Hyperplastic Supernormal'). Since 'innate releasing schemata' are always the '*simplified* characterization of an object or situation' (ibid., vol. 2, 137), abstraction is a fundamental enabling factor for their lock-and-key action.

Tinbergen likewise emphasises that '[a]n animal does not react to all the changes in the environment which its sense organs can receive, but only to *a small part* of them. This is a basic property of instinctive behaviour, the importance of which cannot be stressed too much' (N. Tinbergen, *The Study of Instinct* [Oxford: Oxford University Press, 1974], 25); 'An animal responds "blindly" to only part of the total environmental situation and neglects other parts' (ibid., 27); 'The greater part of the environment has little or no influence, even though the animal may have the sensory equipment for receiving numerous details' (ibid.); 'the animal does not respond to many characteristics of a situation, and that there are but few essential sign stimuli' (ibid., 37). Tinbergen concludes that '[a] releaser in Lorenz's sense is not, in general, that part of an object the animal reacts to, but *those features* of a fellow member of the same species [...] properties— either such of shape and or colour, or special movements, or sounds, or scents, &c.—serving to elicit a response in [...] a fellow member of the same species' (ibid., 56).

Lorenz therefore defines the releaser—his term for '[t]he stimulus-transmission mechanisms which originate in this fashion'—as 'an agent differentiated in the service of the transmission of specific stimuli, which evoke a selective response from the conspecific through a receptor correlate which has been *differentiated in parallel*' (Lorenz, vol. 2, 142, emphasis ours). More specifically, Tinbergen calls 'social releaser' 'a device adapted to release a response in individuals of the same species' or an 'adaptation serving to promote co-operation between the individuals of a conspecific community for the benefit of the group' (Tinbergen, *The Study of Instinct*, 171, 181). He addresses this as a sigint problem for social animals: 'social co-operation depends on the delivery of a signal', and 'in social co-operation of benefit to a community an extra link, that of intercourse between individuals, is inserted between the initiatory perceptual process and the ultimate adaptive response. *This extra link is a kind of signal system.* The signal is given by one individual and it releases the response in one or a number of other individuals. [...] [T]he 'inserted link' is, in a sense, a new feature, and deserves special attention (ibid., 171, emphasis ours).

Again, the 'sign stimuli' involved here 'are always relatively simple and at the same time conspicuous'. 'Social releasers show specialization in the direction of specificity ("improbability")' (ibid.), since evolutionary pressure effectively ushers them toward an information-theoretical optimum, 'a combination of maximal simplicity with maximal general improbability' (Lorenz, *Studies*, vol. 2, 143). The social releaser is subject to selective pressures that tend to increase its abstraction from fine detail, overall gestalt, and extraneous signals native to the environment—what Lorenz calls a '"stimulus-filter effect" (which determines that only these and no other stimuli can produce elicitation)' (ibid., vol 1, 368). Sign stimulus and response mechanism progressively differentiate one another—as Lorenz states quite categorically, '[w]herever an endogenous-automatic motor pattern or an orienting response (or, as usually occurs, a behavioural system based on both elements) has a conspecific as its object, it is *not only the differentiation of the releasing mechanism developed for the object, but also the object itself which is governed by the factors determining the evolution of Species.* [...] The stimulus-receiving apparatus and the stimulus-transmission apparatus are parts of the same organic system, and *both are further differentiated, in connection with their common function of "communication" between conspecifics, in a simultaneous and parallel process.*' (Lorenz, *Studies*, vol. 2, 141, emphasis ours). This differentiation institutes a conventional distance from biological causality narrowly understood: '[W]here an intraspecific system of signal transmitting and signal-receiving differentiation has emerged, the form of the signals is almost exclusively a historical product of "convention" between the stimulus-transmitter and the stimulus-receiver, and there is only a loose relationship with the external environment' (ibid., 143).

What is really missing in the short-lived battle between Tweedledum and Tweedledummer is that cuteness involves a *circuit* in which signals and responses, supply side and demand side, so to speak, co-evolve in a *feedback cycle* of differentiation, and that in the process there emerges 'a kind of signal system' that is *both* subject to natural necessity *and* contingent and conventional (a 'synthetic a priori' of sorts), a system to which it is difficult to assign any 'function' (unless anastrophically...).

More recently, Stephen Levinson has reaffirmed that in this acutification cycle, selection operates on both sign and receptor: 'if parents invest more in "cuter" offspring, their own preferences may be passed on as well as the stimulus that triggers the preference;

similarly, if mates by this mechanism come to prefer "cuter" mates, the process can *accelerate*' (emphasis ours! S.C. Levinson, 'The Interaction Engine: Cuteness Selection and the Evolution of the Interactional Base for Language', *Philosophical Transactions of the Royal Society B* 377 [2022]: 4). Levinson suggests that cuteness might be a 'runaway' phenomenon like the peacock's tail which Darwin thought such 'an awful stretcher' for evolutionary theory—in other words, a phenomenon of natural supernormality produced by an evolutionary feedback circuit extravagating outside of strict survival criteria.

Levinson then makes the plausible suggestion that the evolutionary advantages of 'cuteness selection' ('the evolutionary mechanism coupling appealing features and caring responses') may be related to the 'interaction engine' that drives the transition of *homo sapiens* into social, language-using animals (see S.C. Levinson, 'Interactional Foundations of Language: The Interaction Engine Hypothesis', in P. Hagoort [ed.], *Human Language: From Genes and Brain to Behavior* [Cambridge, MA: MIT Press, 2019], 189–200). On this account cuteness would be a core component in the converging processes of increased sociality and freeing up of resources that enable language acquisition and recognisably human intelligence. Its specific contribution would be made through the promotion of alloparenting, which 'requires a generalization of the maternal relationship, with the mother's interest in the

infant's needs emulated by other adults or older offspring' (ibid., 4). An exaggerated response to cuteness
would enable care and attention to infants to be unlocked from being the sole responsibility of the mother and could be selected for on the basis of its role in
enabling sociality; in turn, 'multiple childhood attachments offered by alloparenting would have facilitated
the acquisition of skills and information crucial to
building cultural adaptations' (ibid., 5). Acutification
leaks out into a broader circuit (see note 155, p186ff)
at the point where subsymbolic affect, become con-
ventionally coded, is invested as a vector of sociality;
if we should still wish to abide by such categories,
Cute exits nature and enters into history.

This would amply address Sanders's suspicion
that, in order to be a significant adaptation, cuteness
would need to do more than merely elicit the nurturing
of infants: Levinson's suggestion is that cuteness con-
tributes to nothing less than a 'possible account for
how humans developed the extended "mind-reading"
that makes language feasible', 'based on the generalization of mother-infant sensitivities, spurred by alloparenting and the possible runaway characteristics
of "cuteness selection"' (ibid., 6). The oxytocin/acc of
cuteness selection, consisting in a social generalisa-
tion of releaser behaviour outside of its narrowly biological function, would then abet the progressive unlocking of social conventional sign use and promote
further 'unnatural' behaviour.

Recent work in cognitive science similarly suggests that 'cuteness ignites activity in metastable brain networks, which provides a framework for sustaining the slowness inherent to prosocial behaviours' (M.L. Kringelbach et al., 'On Cuteness: Unlocking the Parental Brain and Beyond', *Trends in Cognitive Sciences* 20:7 [2016], 545–58: 545), confirming that cuteness's promotion of attention 'enable[s] infants to quickly affect people's, both parents and nonparents, brains and minds, which opens the possibility for complex caregiving and the promotion of sociality. Cuteness, then, displays both instantaneous impacts and gradual effects that aid infants' evolutionary aim of survival, perhaps linked to both proximate and ultimate evolutionary functions' (ibid., 546).

Beyond alloparenting, as 'a general promoter of sociality acting through mentalisation' (ibid., 554), cuteness is not even limited to relations between human conspecifics. This 'signal that elicits both fast and slow brain activity linked to affiliative behaviours [...] is not limited to infants, but can be extended *to other species and even inanimate objects*' (ibid.): it promotes human sociality but also widens its circle beyond the bounds of what is immediately evolutionarily advantageous: 'the anthropomorphising that accompanies cuteness might [even] serve to [...] counteract the dehumanisation and xenophobia all too common in our nature' (ibid., 556).

This sheds light upon yet another conundrum. Tinbergen had argued that the refinement of sign-stimuli into information-dense conventional signs 'is not only a means of guaranteeing the release of specific responses, but […] serves to confine the influence of social releasers to individuals of the same species. Since the great majority of social releasers are developed in the service of reproduction, their specificity causes them to act as reproductive isolation mechanisms' (Tinbergen, *The Study of Instinct*, 184). But Cute is far from being a solely intraspecific phenomenon: before we even get to anime characters and the mess they make of 'reproductive isolation mechanisms' ('By the 10th image dissociation anime girls have become a purely impossible form of womanhood, so impossible yet so lusted for that all standards of womanhood are judged against it as the type specimen', Watts, 'On the Concept of Moé'), how did cats, for instance, end up being *cuter* than human babies? Do the socialising virtues of cuteness explain this surplus value that invites 'intra-species treason' (R. Snedeker, 'The Evolution of Cuteness: Why Kittens and Puppies Beat Babies, Paws Down', *Only Sky*, 2 April 2023, <https://onlysky.media/rsnedeker/the-evolution-of-cuteness-why-kittens-and-puppies-beat-babies-paws-down/>)?

This spillover into animal adoration could perhaps be explained as an accident of mammalian monophyly; we could also posit an asymmetry whereby the releaser receptor is more susceptible to supernormalising than the morphology of the sign stimulus (presumably hacking the nervous system is 'cheaper' than changing facial physiognomy), which would allow the passion for cuteness to outrun the meagre stimulus available from conspecifics.... But we must also consider the intense entanglement, over evolutionarily significant time-frames, between humans and dogs (see M. Alizart, *Dogs*, tr. R. Mackay [Cambridge: Polity, 2019]) and humans and cats (see the internet). Since humans have selectively domesticated and bred these animals for many generations, our captivation by their cuteness is an undecidably 'naturecultural' relay of the acutification process described above, as are the ersatz phyla of Mickey Mouse, dolls, and teddy bears.

In summary, *surrogacy*, *abstraction*, *runaway positive feedback*, and *supernormalisation* were all characteristic of Cute before it hit the market, the factory, and the screen, all of which however serve to accelerate the process further, launching acutification onto a second circuit. The attempted naturalistic reduction of Cute to an evolutionary just-so story via rudimentary evopsych fails to grasp both the bootstrapping dimension of cuteness and the continuity between these different circuits of acutification (see note 155, p186ff).

Neither Darwin nor genetics are an alibi for cultural eliminativism, aesthetic snobbery, or reproductive

conservatism. '[C]uteness goes beyond an atten-
tion-grabbing evolutionary strategy that infants use
to attract care and protection': 'like a Trojan horse,
cuteness opens doors that might otherwise remain
shut' (Kringelbach et al., 556, emphasis ours). Even
from the point of view of evolution, Cute is not a trap,
but a war machine that opens portals.

153.   K. Robinson, 'Our Evolved Minds: Supernormal
Stimuli', *The Web of Life*, <https://www.overstoryalli-
ance.org/library/supernormal-stimuli/>. The coupling
of an evolutionary account and the cultural disparag-
ing of Cute is marked in the critique of John Morreall
(see Morreall, 'The Contingency of Cuteness'; Morreall
and Loy, 'Kitsch and Aesthetic Education').

154.   From bratwurst-denken to Frankfurter misera-
bilism, always Sausage vs. Egg.

155.   We are now in a position to summarise a provi-
sional model in which the historical process takes in
(at least) three relatively autonomous circuits of acutification, each featuring its own mechanisms of acceleration and fitness criteria along with specific fetters
upon its realisation of the Idea that will have been piloting all of this from the future, but which comes only
at the end—the universal, the body without organs
and desiring production—under the conditions determined by an apparently victorious cuteness.

Cute is first discovered within the first circuit, that of 'nature', emerging as a perceptual adumbration constrained by biological limitations. A runaway process of intraspecific co-evolution differentiates a set of rudimentary sign-stimuli (the Kindchenschema) along with corresponding receptors (see note 153, p172ff). Escalation of Cute within this circuit stalls with the attainment of a stable evolutionary strategy, but its rudimentary abstraction and oversensitisation to cute stimuli open the door to functional drift and surrogacy.

The second circuit, that of the 'market', relays the differentiation and honing of cute stimuli in an accelerated culture-industrial cycle of supernormalisation (see note 148, p164ff). Further abstracted from biological function, market forces allow Cute desire to prevail over social-cultural norms, and it enters into experimental couplings with human sexuality. Escalation continues, but capitalist axioms tend to inhibit the process to the extent that they accommodate cultural conservatism, lock onto reified forms of cuteness, and allow profit to trump intensification.

These tendencies are counteracted by the third circuit, 'the database', (see note 133, p156ff). Here the acutification cycle is further accelerated, this time by contracting it into a tighter circuit in which individual consumers and small distributed collectives become incubators for the mutual escalation of stimulus and response, looped through networked digital media and inevitably tending toward autocutification through peak shift and studied refinement. The third circuit draws off the products of the second, which picked up where the first left off, but simultaneously feeds back into it, schooling the market in ever more acutely honed moé-niches.

Circulating within and across these three circuits, Cute progressively discards all manner of residual natural, cultural, sexual, and subjective obstacles to its further intensification, while elaborating new devices and new forms and matters in which it can be experimentally realised.

The fact that Cute is first discovered within the first circuit does not mean that it finds its original model there any more than in the plushy trinkets of late capitalism. When the Kindchenschema releasers took off, quite contingently, on the first circuit, they awakened receptivity to Cute via the model most readily accessible to the biological realm, which already brought with it a certain collateral surplus value. Capitalism opens the field, acting as a search engine (Lorenz's distributed dummy experiment) bounded by certain axiomatic limitations, serving to further decouple the exploitable phase-space of Cute from its biological model while testing it against legacy human culture. In the third circuit, under the conditions of a twenty-first century capitalism marked by a porosity between production and consumption, the e-girls, t-girls, NEETS, anons, and otaku free themselves from

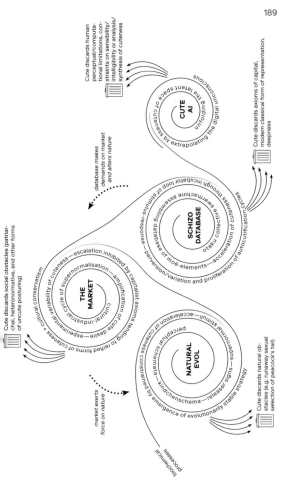

Cute discards human perceptual/computational limitations, constraints on sensibility/intelligibility or analysis/synthesis of cuteness

Cute discards axioms of capital, modern classical form of representation, deepness

Cute discards social obstacles (patriarchal, heteronormative, and other forms of uncute posturing) + cultural conservatism

Cute discards natural obstacles (e.g. runaway sexual selection of peacock's tail)

CUTE AI

Cute discards cuteness by extrapolating the latent space of the digital unconscious

SCHIZO DATABASE

otaku collective swarmachine assembling incubator loop of stimulus-response—perversion/variation and proliferation of autocutification cycles—acceleration of cuteness of moé-elements—database

database makes demands on market and alters nature

THE MARKET

cycle of supernormalisation—amplification of cute desire—experimental variability of cuteness—escalation inhibited by capitalist axioms tending to reified forms of cuteness

cultural-industrial

market exerts force on nature

NATURAL EVOL

perceptual schemata—kinderschema—releaser 'signs'—supernormal stimuli—acceleration of cuteness constrained by emergence of evolutionarily stable strategy

biochemical processes

Circuits of acutification and trajectory of cuteness in possibility space (diagram by Inigo Wilkins)

at least some of the capitalist axioms, schizophreni-
cally accelerate the production-consumption cycle,
and operate as an informal R&D department, testing
ever more piquant formulations on the pink market
that will later enter into general circulation.

We have already warned (see p32 and note
105, p125) that the third circuit should not be under-
estimated, since the desiring-production it incubates
emerges as collective demand on the second circuit,
potentially even initiating processes that will reach
back down into the first circuit to alter the 'natural'
conditions under which it emerged.

We might speculatively suggest a fourth circuit
in which AI becomes a device for further unfolding the
latent spaces of cuteness by extrapolating from the
collective digital unconscious, taking off from the
third circuit by rendering its creations ever more vivid
and responsive while decoupling them more decisive-
ly from residual cultural, social, and sexual prohibitions
and enabling deeper bonds with lifelong virtual companions, producing unprecedented intensifications of
Cute beyond the dreams of even the keenest of yes-
terday's otaku. (On this point, see the work of Bogna
Konior.)

The Idea of Cute, we feel, is ultimately and inti-
mately a problem, a complex of more or less obscurely perceived virtual intensities whose transcendental
shape can be incarnated in various matters as multimodal spatio-temporal dynamisms—plastic, linguistic,

sonic, tactile.... As we draw relatively closer to it, build machines to aid us in enjoying it more acutely, and become more adept at manipulating and navigating its sweet subtleties, as the circuits warm up, Cute gradually reveals the anastrophic sense of its historical acceleration. But there will be no triumphant fanfare, no advent of the Idea in some *geistige* climactic moment of triumphant self-actualisation. Cute doesn't come until the last moment, which it perpetually delays.

156.   R.M. Rilke, 'First Elegy', *Duino Elegies*, tr. D. Young (New York: Norton, 1978), 19. For some astonishing insights on the relation between cuteness, technology, and the angelic, see once again the work of Bogna Konior.

Thanks to our friends, anemones, facilitators, inspirations, and fellow cuties: Éric Alliez, Milia Xin Bi, Bidston Observatory, Chase, Coslimee, DC Barker, Hannah Diamond, Dino Ge Zhang, DJ Benetti, Burt di Rimini, Dragon Maid Committee, Caroline Foley, Felicita, Femboypup, Formless Twins, Griffin, Danny L Harle, Yuk Hui, Sylvia Kastel, Kode9, Bogna Konior, Icky and F1nn, Kris2chrome, Isabel Millar, Thomas Moynihan, Rhea Myers, Nekokuny, Outsieness, Katherine Pickard, Pobbles, Kyary Pamyu Pamyu, Alex Quicho, qwerty_uiop, SaintSunah, Audrey Schmidt, Slimegirl, SOPHIE, SSTRAPP, Patricia Taxxon, Unsound, Natalie Terezi Rei Watts, V and Storm, Terah Walkup, Yonq, Xenogothic.

Special thanks to Inigo Wilkins and Sion Dafwyn for their careful reading and comments.

For Wryly, RIP, thx for all the snuggles.

BOBBLIOGRAPHY

Adkins, Elizabeth Kocher. 'Genes, Hormones, Sex and Gender', in G.W. Barlow and J. Silverberg (eds.), *Sociobiology: Beyond Nature/Nurture*. London: Routledge, 1980. 385–415.

Alexandre, Henri. 'Contribution of the Belgian School of Embryology to the Concept of Neural Induction by the Organizer', *International Journal of Developmental Biology* 45 (2001): 67–72.

Alizart, Marc. *Dogs*, tr. R. Mackay. Cambridge: Polity, 2019.

Alliez, Éric, with Jean-Clet Martin. *The Brain-Eye: New Histories of Modern Painting*, tr. R. Mackay. London and New York: Rowman and Littlefield, 2016.

Alliez, Éric, with Jean-Claude Bonne. *Duchamp Looked At (From the Other Side)/Duchamp With (and Against) Lacan*, tr. R. Mackay and M.B. Kronic. Falmouth: Urbanomic, 2022.

Anonymous. 'Akamatsu-sensei Talks "Moé"', *Matthew's Anime Blog*, 20 July 2005, <https://archives.4-ch.net/anime/kareha.pl/1122583157/>.

Anonymous. 'Amae (甘え) | Manja | Sajiao (撒娇)', *Intercultural Word Sensei*, <https://interculturalwordsensei.org/amae-え-manja-sajiao-撒娇/>.

Anonymous. 'The Substack Sequence', *Effective Accelerationism*, March 2023, <https://www.effectiveacceleration.org/s/fywu-JhWrRmJZPhqky>.

Anonymous. 'Why is Anime and Being Attracted to Fictional Characters Looked Down Upon?', *Asexuality.org*, <https://www.asexuality.org/en/topic/204455-why-is-anime-and-being-attracted-to-fictional-characters-looked-down-upon/>.

Anonymous. 'What Makes Something Cute?: Cute vs Kawaii', *Slap Happy Larry*, January 2023, <https://www.slaphappylarry.com/cute-definition-cute-vs-kawaii/>.

Appel, Toby A. *The Cuvier-Geoffroy Debate: French Biology in the Decades Before Darwin*. New York and Oxford: Oxford University Press, 1987.

Aragón, Oriana R., Margaret S. Clark, Rebecca L. Dyer, and John A. Bargh. 'Dimorphous Expressions of Positive Emotion: Displays of Both Care and Aggression in Response to Cute Stimuli', *Psychological Science* 26:3 (2015): 259–73.

Avanessian, Armen, and Robin Mackay (eds.). *#accelerate: The Accelerationist Reader*. Falmouth and Berlin: Urbanomic/Merve, 2014.

Azuma, Hiroki. 'Super Flat Speculation', in T. Murakami, *Superflat*. Tokyo: Madra, 2000. 138–51.

——— 'The Animalization of Otaku Culture'. Y. Furahata and M. Steinberg (tr.). *Mechademia* 2 (2007): 175–87.

——— *Otaku: Japan's Database Animals*. J.E. Abel and Shion Kono (tr.). Minneapolis: University of Minnesota Press, 2009.

Ballard, J.G. *Extreme Metaphors: Interviews with J.G. Ballard 1967–2008*. D. O'Hara and S. Sellars (eds.). New York: HarperCollins, 2012.

Balzac, Honoré de. 'Guide-Âne a l'usage des animaux qui veulent parvenir aux honneurs', in P.-J Stahl, *Scènes de la vie privée et publique des animaux*. Paris: J. Hetzel et Paulin, 1842. 183–208.

Barron, Andrew B., and Brian Hare. 'Prosociality and a Sociosexual Hypothesis for the Evolution of Same-Sex Attraction in Humans', *Frontiers in Psychology* 10:2955 (2020).

Berger, Edmund. 'Unconditional Acceleration and the Question Of Praxis: Some Preliminary Thoughts', *Synthetic Zero*, March 2017, <https://syntheticzero.net/2017/03/28/unconditional-acceleration-and-the-question-of-praxis-some-preliminary-thoughts/ #comment-30191>.

——— 'Synthetic Fabrication: The Myth of the Politics-to-Come (Part 0: Introduction)', *Vast Abrupt*, January 2018, <https://vastabrupt.com/2018/01/12/synthetic-fabrication-pt0/>.

Brassier, Ray. Untitled presentation, <https://moskvax.wordpress.com/2010/ 09/30/accelerationism-ray-brassier/>.

Brzozowska-Brywczyńska, Maja. 'Monstrous/Cute. Notes on the Ambivalent Nature of Cuteness', in N. Scott (ed.), *Monsters and the Monstrous: Myths and Metaphors of Enduring Evil*. Amsterdam/New York: Rodopi 2007. 213–27.

Burroughs, William Jr. *Speed*. Woodstock, NY: Overlook Press, 1984.

Cahn, Théophile. *La Vie et l'oeuvre d'Étienne Geoffroy Saint-Hilaire*. Paris: PUF, 1962.

Canguilhem, Georges. *Knowledge of Life*, tr. S. Geroulanos and D. Ginsburg. New York: Fordham University Press, 2008.

Caplan, Arthur L.. 'A Critical Examination of Current Sociobiological Theory: Adequacy and Implications', in Barlow and Silverberg (eds.), *Sociobiology: Beyond Nature/Nurture*. 97–114.

Carpi, Giancarlo. 'The Human in the Fetish of the Human. Cuteness in Futurist Cinema, Literature, and Visual Arts', in Rossella Catanese (ed.), *Futurist Cinema: Studies on Italian Avant-garde Film*. Amsterdam: Amsterdam University Press, 2017. 115–29.

Carroll, Lewis. *Through the Looking-Glass, And What Alice Found There*. London: Macmillan, 1872.

———— *Sylvie and Bruno*. London: Macmillan, 1889.

———— *Sylvie and Bruno Concluded*. London: Macmillan, 1893.

Ccru, 'The Excruciation of Hummpa-Taddum', in *Writings 1997–2003*. Falmouth and Shanghai: Urbanomic/Time Spiral, 2017. 97–9.

Chen, Elsie. 'Chinese Millennials Are "Chilling", and Beijing Isn't Happy About It', *The New York Times*, <https://www.nytimes.com/2021/07/03/world/asia/china-slackers-tangping.html>.

Chu, Andrea Long. *Females*. London: Verso, 2019.

Collet, Sandra. 'The Evolution of Social Species in Balzac's Comédie Humaine', in *Biological Time, Historical Time: Transfers and Transformations in 19th Century Literature (Faux Titre 431)*. Leiden: Brill, 2018. 241–57.

Cuboniks, Laboria. 'Xenofeminism: A Politics for Alienation', 2015, <https://laboriacuboniks.net/manifesto/>.

Dalcq, Albert. *Form and Causality in Early Development*. Cambridge: Cambridge University Press, 1938.

———— *L'Œuf et son dynamisme organisateur*. Paris: Albin Michel, 1941.

———— *Introduction to General Embryology*, tr. J. Medawar. Oxford: Oxford University Press, 1957.

Dale, Joshua. 'The Appeal of the Cute Object: Desire, Domestica-
    tion, and Agency' in J. Dale, J. Goggin, J. Leda, A. P. MacIntyre
    and D. Negra (eds.), *The Aesthetics and Affects of Cuteness*.
    New York and London: Routledge, 2017. 35–55.

Dawkins, Richard. 'Good Strategy or Evolutionarily Stable Strate-
    gy?', in Barlow and Silverberg (eds.). *Sociobiology: Beyond Na-
    ture/Nurture*. 331–69.

———— *The Selfish Gene: 40th Anniversary Edition*. Oxford: Ox-
    ford University Press, 2016.

'DC Barker'. 'Scattered Thoughts on Cute/Acc', *Psuedoanalysis*,
    <https://psuedoanalysis.blogspot.com/2020/08/scat-
    tered-thoughts- on-cuteacc.html>.

Dean, Aria. 'Notes on Blacceleration', *e-flux* 87 (December 2017), <
    https://www.e-flux.com/journal/87/169402/notes-on-blac-
    celeration/>.

Delacroix, Eugène. *The Journal of Eugène Delacroix*, tr. L. Norton.
    Ithaca, NY: Cornell University Press, 1980.

———— *Journal (1822–1863)*. Paris: Plon, 1996.

Deleuze, Gilles. 'Bartleby; Or, The Formula', in *Essays Critical and Clin-
    ical*, tr. D.W. Smith and M.A. Greco. London: Verso, 1998. 68–90.

———— *Instincts and Institutions*. Paris: Hachette, 1953.

———— 'Desert Islands', in D. Lapoujade (ed.), *Desert Islands and
    Other Texts 1953–1974*. Los Angeles: Semiotext(e), 2004. 9–14.

———— 'On Gilbert Simondon', in D. Lapoujade (ed.), *Desert Is-
    lands and Other Texts 1953–1974*. Los Angeles: Semiotext(e),
    2004. 86–9.

———— and Félix Guattari. *A Thousand Plateaus*, tr. B. Massumi.
    Minneapolis: University of Minnesota Press, 1987.

————— and Félix Guattari. *Anti-Oedipus: Capitalism and Schizophrenia*, tr. R. Hurley, M. Seem, and H.R. Lane. Minneapolis: University of Minnesota Press, 1983.

————— *Difference and Repetition*, tr. P. Patton. New York: Columbia University Press, 1994.

————— *Logic of Sense*, tr. M. Lester and C. Stivale. New York: Columbia University Press, 1993.

————— *Nietzsche and Philosophy*, tr. H. Tomlinson. London and New York: Continuum, 2002.

————— *Proust and Signs: The Complete Text*, tr. R. Howard. London: Athlone, 2000.

De Seta, Gabriele. '"Meng? It Just Means Cute": A Chinese Online Vernacular Term in Context', *M/C Journal* 17:2 (2014), <https://www.journal.media-culture.org.au/index.php/mcjournal/article/view/789>.

Eliade, Mircea. *Rites and Symbols of Initiation*, tr. Willard R. Trask. New York: Harper Colophon, 1958.

————— 'Time and Eternity in Indian Thought', in J. Campbell (ed.), *Man and Time: Papers from the Eranos Yearbooks*. Princeton, NJ: Princeton University Press, 1983. 173–90.

Ferro, Shaunacy. 'Why Do We Want to Squeeze Cute Things?', *Popular Science*, 25 January 2013, <https://www.popsci.com/science/article/2013-01/science-says-adorable-animals-turn-us-aggressive/>.

Fisher, Mark. 'Continuous Contact', *k-punk*, 23 January 2005, <http://k-punk.org/continuous-contact/>.

————— *Flatline Constructs: Gothic Materialism and Cybernetic Theory-Fiction*. New York: Exmiliary Collective, 2018.

Foucault, Michel. 'Introduction', *Herculine Barbin: Being the Recently Discovered Memoirs of a Nineteenth-Century French Hermaphrodite*, tr. R. McDougall. New York: Vintage, 2010.

Galbraith, Patrick W. (ed). *The Moé Manifesto: An Insider's Look at the Worlds of Manga, Anime, and Gaming*. Tokyo: Tuttle, 2014.

——— 'Moé: Exploring Virtual Potential in Post-Millennial Japan', *Electronic Journal of Contemporary Japanese Studies*, October 2009, <http://www.japanesestudies.org.uk/articles/2009/Galbraith.html>.

Garton, Vincent. 'Unconditional Accelerationism as Antipraxis', *Cyclonotrope*, June 2027, <https://cyclonotrope.wordpress.com/2017/06/12/unconditional-accelerationism-as-antipraxis/>.

Geoffroy Saint-Hilaire, Étienne. *Études progressives d'un naturaliste*. Paris: Roret, 1835.

Goddard, Jean-Christophe. *A Scabby Black Brazilian*. Falmouth: Urbanomic, 2023.

Gould, Stephen Jay. 'Sociobiology and the Theory of Natural Selection', in Barlow and Silverberg (eds.), *Sociobiology: Beyond Nature/Nurture*. 257–72.

——— 'A Biological Homage to Mickey Mouse'. *Ecotone* 4:1–2 (2008): 333–40.

Grant, Iain Hamilton. 'Black Ice', in J.B. Dixon and E. Cassidy (eds.), *Virtual Futures: Cyberotics, Technology, and Post-Human Pragmatism*. London and New York: Routledge, 1998. 132–43.

Grelet, Gilles. *Theory of the Solitary Sailor*. Falmouth: Urbanomic, 2022.

Griaule, Marcel, and Germaine Dieterlen. *The Pale Fox*, tr. S.C. Infantino. Chino Valley, AZ: Continuum Foundation, 1986.

Guattari, Félix. 'Tokyo, the Proud', in G. Genosko and J. Hetrick (eds.), *Machinic Eros: Writings on Japan*. Minneapolis: Univocal, 2015. 13–16.

Harris, Daniel. *Cute, Quaint, Hungry and Romantic, The Aesthetics of Consumerism*. New York: Basic Books, 2000.

Higashimura, Hikaru. 'The Moé Studies Research Circle', in Galbraith (ed.), *The Moé Manifesto*. 136–43.

Honda, Masuko. 'The Genealogy of the Hirahira: Liminality and the Girl', in Tomoko Aoyama and B. Hartley (eds.), *Girl Reading Girl in Japan*. New York: Routledge, 2010. 19–37.

Honda, Toru. 'I May Not be Popular but I Live On', *Frogkun*, 24 November 2016, <https://frogkun.com/2016/11/24/i-may-not-be-popular-but-i-live-on/>.

——— 'The Love Revolution is Here', in Galbraith (ed.), *The Moé Manifesto*. 116–25.

Howie, Elizabeth. 'Indulgence and Refusal: Cuteness, Asceticism, and the Aestheticization of Desire', in J. Boyle and W. Kao (eds.), *The Retro-Futurism of Cuteness*. Brooklyn, NY: Punctum, 2017. 53–66.

Ito, Go. 'The Pleasure of Lines', in Galbraith (ed.), *The Moé Manifesto*. 163–69.

Ito, Noizi. 'Girl Drawing Girl: On Bishōjo Games', in Galbraith (ed.), *The Moé Manifesto*. 109–115.

Jouffroy, Alain. *Marcel Duchamp*. Paris: Centre Georges Pompidou/Dumerchez, 1997.

Jen Boyle and W-C. Kao. 'Introduction: The Time of the Child', in J. Boyle and Wan-Chuan Kao (eds.), *The Retro-Futurism of Cuteness*. Brooklyn, NY: Punctum, 2017. 13–27.

Karhulahti Velli-Matti, and Tanja Välisalo. 'Fictosexuality, Fictoromance, and Fictophilia: A Qualitative Study of Love and Desire for Fictional Characters', *Frontiers in Psychology* 11 (Jan 2021).

Kenji the Enji. 'On Denpa', *On the Ones*, 29 June 2019, <https://ontheones.wordpress.com/2019/06/29/>.

Kerslake, Christian. *Deleuze and the Unconscious*. London and New York: Continuum, 2007.

Kinsella, Sharon. 'Cuties in Japan', in *Women, Media, and Consumption in Japan*, L. Skov and B. Moéran (eds.). Oxford: Curzon Press, 1995. 220–54.

Konior, Bogna. 'The Impersonal Within Us', *Chaosmotics*, <https://www.chaosmotics.com/en/featured/the-impersonal-within-us>.

Kringelbach, Morten L., Eloise A. Stark, Catherine Alexander, Marc H. Bornstein, and Alan Stein. 'On Cuteness: Unlocking the Parental Brain and Beyond', *Trends in Cognitive Sciences* 20: 7 (2016): 545–58.

Kronic, Maya B. Entry 'Egg' in 'Glossalalary' in E. Alliez with J.-C. Bonne, *Duchamp Looked At (From the Other Side)/Duchamp With (and Against) Lacan*, tr. R. Mackay and M.B. Kronic. Falmouth: Urbanomic, 2022. A279/B246.

Lacan, Jacques. 'Problèmes cruciaux pour la psychanalyse. Compte rendu du séminaire 1964–1965', in *Autres Écrits*. Paris: Seuil, 2001.

Land, Nick. 'Circuitries', in *Fanged Noumena*. Falmouth and New York: Urbanomic/Sequence Press, 2011. 289–318.

——— 'Making it with Death: Remarks on Thanatos and Desiring-Production', in *Fanged Noumena*. 261–87.

——— and Sadie Plant. 'Cyberpositive' [1994], in Avanessian and Mackay (eds.), *#accelerate*. 305–13: 305.

Lang, Alexandria Amelia. 'Re-envisioning the Natural World in Eugène Delacroix's Lion Devouring a Horse', MA Thesis, Dept. of Art and Art History, University of Utah, 2016.

Lavery, Grace. 'Egg Theory's Early Style', *Transgender Studies Quarterly* 7:3 (2020): 383–98.

Levinson, Steven C. 'The Interaction Engine: Cuteness Selection and the Evolution of the Interactional Base for Language', *Philosphical Transactions of the Royal Society B* 377 (2022).

———— 'Interactional Foundations of Language: The Interaction Engine Hypothesis', in P. Hagoort (ed.), *Human Language: From Genes and Brain to Behavior*. Cambridge, MA: MIT Press, 2019. 189–200.

Lorenz, Konrad. *Studies in Animal and Human Behaviour*, tr. R. Martin. Cambridge, MA: Harvard University Press, 2 vols., 1971.

Lovecraft, H.P. *Selected Letters 1925–1929*, ed. A. Derleth and D. Wandrei. Sauk City, WI: Arkham House, 1968.

———— 'The Call of Cthulhu', in *H.P. Lovecraft Omnibus 3: The Haunter of the Dark*. London: Voyager, 2000. 61–98.

Lyotard, Jean-François. 'Desirevolution', in Avanessian and Mackay (eds.), *#accelerate*. 243–47.

———— *Libidinal Economy*, tr. I.H. Grant. Bloomington and Indianapolis: Indiana University Press, 1993.

Mackay, Robin. 'Hyperplastic Supernormal', in P. Rosenkranz, *Our Product*. Kassel and London: Fridericianum/Koenig Books, 2017. <https://readthis.wtf/writing/hyperplastic-supernormal/>.

Marcus, Aaron, Masaaki Kurosu, Xiaojuan Ma, Ayako Hashizume. 'Introduction' to Marcus, Aaron, Masaaki Kurosu, Xiaojuan Ma, Ayako Hashizume (eds.), *Cuteness Engineering: Designing Adorable Products and Services*. Cham: Springer, 2017.

May, Simon. *The Power of Cute*. Princeton, NJ: Princeton University Press, 2019.

McGroot, Adolph. 'All Hail the Blessed Sutcliffe', *Whorecull* 1, January 2001, <https://web.archive.org/web/20040614225256/http://www.cinestatic.com/whorecull/issue1/adolph.asp>.

Merish, Lori. 'Cuteness and Commodity Aesthetics: Tom Thumb and Shirley Temple', in *Freakery: Cultural Spectacles of the Extraordinary Body*, ed. R. Garland-Thomson. New York: New York University Press, 1996. 185–203.

Meta-nomad. 'Z/Acc Primer', *jdemeta.net*, 11 January 2019, <https://jdemeta.net/2019/01/11/z-acc-primer/>.

Mina, An Xiao. 'Batman, Pandaman and the Blind Man: A Case Study in Social Change Memes and Internet Censorship in China', *Journal of Visual Culture* 13:3 (2014): 359–75.

Momoi, Halko. 'The Voice of Moé Asks for Understanding: The Struggle against Gender Norms', in Galbraith (ed.), *The Moé Manifesto*. 73–79.

Monden, Masafumi. 'Being Alice in Japan: Performing a Cute, "Girlish" Revolt', *Japan Forum* 26:2 (2014): 265–85.

Morinaga, Takuro. 'For Love or Money: A Lesson in Moé Economics' in Galbraith (ed.), *The Moé Manifesto*. 28–35.

Morreall, John. 'Cuteness', *The British Journal of Aesthetics* 31:1 (January 1991): 39–47.

——— 'The Contingency of Cuteness: A Reply to Sanders', *The British Journal of Aesthetics* 33:3 (July 1993): 283–5.

——— and Jessica Loy. 'Kitsch and Aesthetic Education', *The Journal of Aesthetic Education* 23:4 (1989): 63–73.

Moynihan, Thomas. *Spinal Catastrophism: A Secret History*. Falmouth: Urbanomic, 2020.

Murakami, Takashi. 'The Super Flat Manifesto', in *Superflat*. Tokyo: Madra, 2000. 4–5.

Myers, Rhea. 'Necronomicon', in *Proof of Work: Blockchain Provocations 2011–2021*. Falmouth: Urbanomic, 2022. 242–3.

n1x. 'Gender Acceleration: A Blackpaper'. *Vast Abrupt*, 31 October 2018, <https://vastabrupt.com/2018/10/31/gender-acceleration/>.

Negarestani, Reza. 'A Good Meal', in *Abducting the Outside: Collected Writings 2003–2018*. Falmouth and New York: Urbanomic/Sequence Press, 2024.

Ngai, Sianne. *Our Aesthetic Categories: Zany, Cute, Interesting*. Cambridge, MA and London: Harvard University Press, 2012.

Nguyen, An. 'Eternal Maidens: Kawaii Aesthetics and Otome Sensibility in Lolita Fashion', *East Asian Journal of Popular Culture* 2:1 (2016): 15–31.

Nietzsche, Friedrich. The Will to Power, tr. W. Kaufmann and R. J. Hollingdale. New York: Vintage, 1968.

———— *Sämtliche Werke: Kritische Studienausgabe im 15 Bänden*, ed. G. Colli and M. Montinari. Berlin: De Gruyter, 15 vols., 1988.

———— *Thus Spoke Zarathustra*, tr. A. Del Caro. Cambridge: Cambridge University Press, 2006.

Nittono, Hiroshi. 'The Two-layer Model of "Kawaii": A Behavioural Science Framework for Understanding Kawaii and Cuteness', *East Asian Journal of Popular Culture* 2:1 (2016): 79–95.

NTU-Otastudy Group. 'Fictosexual Manifesto', <https://vocal.media/humans/fictosexual-manifesto>.

O'Sullivan, Simon. *Art Encounters Deleuze and Guattari*. Basingstoke: Palgrave Macmillan, 2006.

Oliver, Mathieu Alemany. 'Consumer Neoteny: An Evolutionary Perspective on Childlike Behavior in Consumer Society', *Evolutionary Psychology* (2016): 1–11.

Ovid, *Metamorphoses*, tr. A.S. Kline, 2000, <https://www.poetryintranslation.com/PITBR/Latin/Metamorph4.php>.

Palau Marti, Montserrat. *Les Dogons*. Paris: PUF, 1957.

Parzival. 'Love is Dead, Long Live the Otaku', *Artificial Night Sky*, <https://artificialnightsky.neocities.org/honda-san/kimomen>.

Perrier, Edmond. *The Philosophy of Zoology Before Darwin*, tr. A. McBirney. Dordrecht: Springer, 2009.

Plant, Sadie. *Zeros and Ones: Digital Women and the New Technoculture*. New York: Doubleday, 1997.

——— 'Coming Across the Future', in J.B. Dixon and E. Cassidy (eds.), *Virtual Futures: Cyberotics, Technology, and Post-Human Pragmatism*. London: Routledge, 1998. 39–47.

Poincaré, Henri. *Science and Hypothesis: The Complete Text*, tr. M. Frappier, A. Smith, and D.J. Stump. London and New York: Bloomsbury, 2018.

Quicho, Alex. 'Everyone is a Girl Online', *Wired*, 11 September 2023, <https://www.wired.com/story/girls-online-culture/>.

——— 'Prey Mode: Why Girls are Pretending to be Cute Animals Online', *Dazed Digital*, 20 November 2023, <https://www.dazeddigital.com/life-culture/article/61336/1/going-prey-mode-girls-cute-animals-online-canthal-tilt-tiktok>.

Richard, Frances. 'Fifteen Theses on the Cute: A Crucial Absence', *Cabinet*, Fall 2001, <https://www.cabinetmagazine.org/issues/4/richard.php>.

Rilke, Rainer Maria. *Duino Elegies*, tr. David Young. New York: Norton, 1978.

Robinson, Keegan. 'Our Evolved Minds: Supernormal Stimuli', *The Web of Life*, <https://www.overstoryalliance.org/library/supernormal-stimuli/>.

Roffe, Jon. 'The Egg: Deleuze Between Darwin and Ruyer', in M.J. Benett and T.S. Posteraro, *Deleuze and Evolutionary Theory*. Edinburgh: Edinburgh University Press, 2019. 42–58.

Saitō, Tamaki. *Beautiful Fighting Girl*, tr. J. Keith Vincent and D. Lawson. Minneapolis: Minnesota University Press, 2011.

Sanders, John T. 'On "Cuteness"', *The British Journal of Aesthetics* 32:2 (April 1992): 162–65.

Satoshi, Kawasaki. カメの甲羅はあばら骨. Tokyo: SB Creative, 2019.

Sauvagnargues, Anne. 'The Wasp and the Orchid', in P. de Assis and P. Guidici (eds.), *Aberrant Nuptials: Deleuze and Artistic Research 2.* Leuven: Leuven University Press , 2019. 177–82.

Shin, Sangah. 'Why Am I Torn Between Surrender and Mastery When it Comes to Cuteness?' *Some Archive #1.* Lucerne: Präsens Editionen, 2019.

Shiokawa, Kanako. 'Cute but Deadly: Women and Violence in Japanese Comics'. J.A. Lent (ed.), *Themes and Issues in Asian Cartooning: Cute, Cheap, Mad, and Sexy.* Bowling Green, OH: Bowling Green State University Popular Press, 1999. 93–125.

Sholtz, Janae. *The Invention of a People: Heidegger and Deleuze on Art and the Political.* Edinburgh: Edinburgh University Press, 2015.

Singleton, Benedict. 'Maximum Jailbreak', in Avanessian and Mackay (eds.), *#accelerate.* 489–507.

Snedeker, Rick. 'The Evolution of Cuteness: Why Kittens and Puppies Beat Babies, Paws Down', *Only Sky*, 2 April 2023, <https://onlysky.media/rsnedeker/>.

Soda, Mitsuru. 'The Philomoé Association: Discours de la moé-thode', in Galbraith (ed.), *The Moé Manifesto*. 145–51.

Snicek, Nick, and Alex Williams. 'Manifesto for an Accelerationist Politics', in Avanessian and Mackay (eds.), *#accelerate*. 347–62.

Stavropolous, Katherine K.M., and L.A. Alba. '"It's So Cute I Could Crush It!" Understanding Neural Mechanisms of Cute Aggression', *Frontiers in Behavioral Neuroscience* 12 (2018).

Steinberg, Neil. 'When Cuteness Comes of Age', *The New Republic*, 16 July 2016, <https://newrepublic.com/article/135244/cuteness-comes-age>.

Stillwell, Echidna. 'The Vault of Murmurs', in Ccru, *Writings 1997–2003*. Falmouth and Shanghai: Urbanomic/Time Spiral, 2017. 65–71.

Stivale, Charles. 'VirtFut3', *driftline.org* (1994). <http://www.driftline.org/cgi-bin/archive/archive_msg.cgi?file=spoon-archives/deleuze-guattari.archive/d-g_1994/deleuze_May.94&msgnum=31 &start=1731&end=2001>.

Thieffry, Denis. 'Rationalizing Early Embryogenesis in the 1930s: Albert Dalcq on Gradients and Fields', *Journal of the History of Biology* 34 (2001): 149–81.

Thom, René. *Structural Stability and Morphogenesis*, tr. D.H. Fowler. Reading, MA: W.A. Benjamin, 1975.

Tinbergen, Nikolaas. *The Study of Instinct*. Oxford: Oxford University Press, 1974.

Tiqqun. *Raw Materials for a Theory of the Young-Girl*, tr. A. Reines. Los Angeles: Semiotext(e), 2001.

———— *Raw Materials for a Theory of the Young-Girl* (with 1999 Introduction), <https://files.libcom.org/files/jeune-fille.pdf>.

Treat, John Whittier. 'Yoshimoto Banana Writes Home: The Shōjo in Japanese Popular Culture', in J.W. Treat (ed.), *Contemporary Japan and Popular Culture*. Honolulu: University of Hawai'i Press, 1996. 275–308.

——— 'Yoshimoto Banana's Kitchen, or the Cultural Logic of Japanese Consumerism', in L. Skov and B. Moeran (eds.), *Women Media and Consumption in Japan*. London and New York: Routledge, 2013. 274–98.

Waldman, Katie. 'The Totally Adorable History of Cute', *Slate*, February 2015, <https://slate.com/human-interest/2015/02/cute-etymology-and-history-from-sharp-keen-or-shrewd-to-charming-and-attractive.html>.

Watts, Natalie Terezi Rei. 'On the Concept of Moé', *Urbanomic Documents*, 2021, <https://www.urbanomic.com/document/moe/>.

Webster, George. 'The Metaphysics Science Needs: Deleuze's Naturalism', *European Journal of Philosophy* 2023: 1–27.

Wilson, Edward O. 'A Consideration of the Genetic Foundation of Human Social Behaviour', in Barlow and Silverberg (eds.), *Sociobiology: Beyond Nature/Nurture*. 295–304.

Wittkower, Dylan E. 'On the Origins of the Cute as a Dominant Aesthetic Category in Digital Culture', in T.W. Luke and J. Hunsinger (eds.), *Putting Knowledge to Work and Letting Information Play*. Rotterdam: SensePublishers, 2012. 212–21.

Yueh, Hsin-I Sydney. 'Body Performance in Gendered Language: Deconstructing the Mandarin Term Sajiao in the Cultural Context of Taiwan', *Journal of Theories and Research in Education* 8:1 (2013): 159–82.

INDEGGS

2.5D (Honda Toru) 37, 149
2chan 144

A

abstraction 154, 156, 160, 164,
    165, 176, 185, 187
    and partial objects 154
    and releasers 176–179
accelerationism, acceleration
    4–6, 7, 16, 18, 27, 32, 51, 69,
    100, 109, 186, 191
    blaccelerationism (bl/acc) 70
    cute (cute/acc) 4, 5, 18, 45,
        46, 50, 51, 80, 109
    synonymy of cute with 5, 18,
        32, 45–46
    effective (e/acc) 70
    gender (g/acc) 69
    in Nietzsche 151
    left (l/acc) 5, 51, 69
    Male Fantasy and 30
    plurality of 7
    regression and 5, 100
    right (r/acc) 51, 70
    singularity and 52
    surrender and 6
    trans communities and 124
    sexuality and 86
    transcendental and 100
    unconditional (u/acc) 52, 69
    zero (z/acc) 70
acutification 164, 180, 185
    circuits of 94, 124, 149, 164,

    165, 171, 182, 185, 186–191
    and identification 94
adolescence 112, 119, 122
Adorno, Theodor W. (Hippo King
    Archibald) 165
aegyo 10, 12, 20, 81, 91–92
aesthetics 11, 172
agency 125, 158, 166
    and guilt 158
aggression 17, 18
AI 144, 157, 190
    and sexting 144, 157
    as fourth circuit of
        acutification 190
Alice (Carroll) 83
Alliez, Éric 106
anamnesis 54, 64, 67
anastrophe 6, 44, 69, 180, 191
anatomy
    comparative 96, 98–99
    philosophical (Geoffroy) 103
animals 26, 39, 92, 98, 100, 101,
    102, 105, 106, 153, 177–178,
    184–185
    animalisation (Azuma) 154
    flat 35, 141
    sexuality and 85
    transcendental 78
anime 39, 76, 78, 119, 141–142,
    146, 147–148, 171, 184
    and trauma 141–142
An Xiao Mina 79
aphaeresis 10, 72

212

apocalypse 3
art 73–74, 165–166
    'trash art' 164
artificiality, artificialisation 73, 91,
    120, 152, 169, 170
    aegyo and 91
asceticism 15, 84
asexuality 146
authenticity 33, 127, 164
auto-cutification 39, 94, 188 *see
    also* object, self-objectifica-
    tion
autophilia 94
avatars 92
Azuma, Hiroki 37, 78, 84, 153–154,
    155, 156–157

B

babies *see* infants
baby talk *see* speech
Ballard, J.G. 85, 90
Balzac, Honoré de 104–105
Barker, Daniel 95
Bartleby (Melville) 151
beauty 11, 72
becoming 24, 25, 27, 33, 102, 108,
    123
becoming-girl 24
becoming-woman 108
Berger, Edmund 69
biology 25–26, 26, 97, 99, 100,
    180, 188
birth
    second 53, 65, 88, 159
bluntness 87, 95
body 25, 30, 31, 33, 41, 108, 109
    abstraction of 160
    animal 26
    cute 14
    gender and 33, 39

moé and 39, 145, 155
organic 161–160
socialisation and 110
virtual 30, 33, 109–110
body without organs (BwO) 59,
    66, 90, 101, 108, 109, 125, 186
boy 83, 108, 144
brain 183
Brassier, Ray 69
breedability 4, 31
burriko 81
Burroughs, William 3, 50
bussy 102

C

capitalism, capital 4, 11, 18, 43,
    113, 120, 121, 122, 123, 125,
    130–133, 134, 135, 137, 138, 148,
    187, 188, 190
    McGroot on 137–138
    antimarkets and 124
    conservatism of 187
    contradictory tendencies of
        18, 88
    fiction and, Mark Fisher on
        148
    love capitalism 150
    shōjo and 113
    women and 131–133, 137–138
caretaking 17, 183
Carroll, Lewis 9, 23, 81, 83–82, 88
catastrophe
    vs. anastrophe 69
catboys 6, 25
cats 23, 38, 150, 184, 185, 192
    cat ears 23, 37
    cute cat theory (Ethan
        Zuckerman) 79
Ccru 80
chatbots 157

Child, Charles Manning 55
children 75–76, 150, 166, 170, 182
    see also infants
China 79, 148, 149
chonk 18
Cixin, Liu 84
climax 16, 86, 191
clothing 24, 110, 149
    and shōjo 115
coincidence 53, 144
collectivity, collectives 33
    AI and 144, 190
    database and 79, 157
    in kawaii culture 115
    moé culture and 147
    on third circuit of acutification
        187
    on second circuit of
        acutification 190
    technology and 32
    trans 124
    transformation and 30, 124
commodities 43, 77, 78, 94, 132,
    135, 140, 166
compactness 18–19
consumer, consumerism,
    consumption 20, 31, 42, 44, 77,
    119, 137, 146, 163
    shōjo and 113, 118
consummation 15, 18
contagion 10, 12, 27, 32, 139 *see
    also* cutagion
contingency 155
    in evolution 153
    of cuteness 174, 188
    of moé 37, 155
    of releasers 180
cosmogony
    Dogon 60–63
counteractualisation 26, 27, 30

COVID-19 49
cringe
    and aegyo 91
critique 41, 43, 159, 163
    Adorno and 165
    desire and 159
    Kantian 161–162
crush 18
Cuboniks, Laboria 69
cuddles 13, 19
cunning 12, 79, 116
cutagion 21, 40
cute
    etymology of 9–13, 73, 87
    as process 162
    as accelerationist stance 4–5
    as Idea 1, 187, 190
    as oxymoron 95
    as problem 1, 12, 42, 190
    as war machine 186
    as acceleration 32
    has no interiority 13, 14, 20, 33
    is anticlimactic 16, 191
    is excessive 11, 17, 18, 73, 82,
        88
    is not an object 42–43
    transcendental shape of 12,
        190
Cuvier, Jean Léopold Nicolas
    Frédéric 25–27, 96–97, 98, 99,
    100, 101–100, 103, 104
cyberpunk
    trans communities as 124

D
Dalcq, Albert 55–58, 59, 63, 64,
    99
dark forest (Liu Cixin) 84
Darwin, Charles 181

database (Hiroki Azuma) 37–40, 79, 154, 156–157, 160, 187–188
'DC Barker' 51
Dean, Aria 70
degeneracy 30, 32, 44
Delacroix, Eugène 106
Deleuze, Franny 29
Deleuze, Gilles 35, 50, 54, 169
    on Bartleby 151
    on eggs 54–58, 99
    on instincts and institutions 169
    on Lewis Carroll 83
demons 4, 6, 7, 144
denpa 143–144
Densha Otoko 142–144
desire 159–160
    2D 36
    and identification 94
    and moé 147
    and repression 159
    and revolution 68, 157
    and shame 159
    anomalous 124
Dieterlen, Germaine 60
difference 26, 97
differentiation 57, 60, 86, 109, 115, 159, 164, 166, 175, 178–180, 187
two-dimensionality see flatness
disciplinarity 1, 162
dogs 185
domesticity, domestication
    and Capital, McGroot on 137–138
    and the Young-Girl 136–137, 140
    of shōjo 121
dreams 32, 67
drives 15, 16, 18, 25, 43, 44

confusion of, in cute aggression 17
Duchamp, Marcel 20, 93

E
eating 20
eggs 5, 14, 27, 31, 32, 53–66, 82, 98–99, 103, 109, 109–110, 125, 186
    cosmic 32, 53, 60, 125
    cracking of 124
    database and 38
    Dogon 59, 60–63
    metaphysical error and 162
    long and short, conversion of 103
    moé and 39
    technology and 125
    trans 65
Eliade, Mircea 53, 62
embarrassment 32
embryology, embryo 54–59, 63–68
    in Geoffroy 98–100
error
    and evolution 171–172
    erotic target location 44
    metaphysical 161–162
escape 32, 124
eschatology 52
etymology 10, 87
euphoria 27, 124
evolution 42, 152, 172–186
    and error 171–172
    cultural 171
evolutionarily stable strategy (ESS) 167, 175, 187
evolutionary psychology 43–44, 166–170

eyes 12, 166
    in manga 115

F

fantasy 32, 36, 78, 130, 133
fashion
    2D 149
    cute, in Japan 122
fate map 50, 57–58
feedback 30, 153, 164, 180, 181, 185
    negative 87
    positive 30, 32, 164, 185
femboys 24, 29
femininity 94
    and moé 40–44
feminism 131
    mcGroot on 137
fiction 37, 160
    and capitalism, Mark Fisher on 148
    and reality 36, 147, 160
fictosexuality 146
fingers 95
fixed action patterns 16
flatness 14, 20, 35, 37, 84, 92, 150
    acceleration and, in Nietzsche 151–152
    fashion and 149
    flatmaxxing 39, 149
    geometry and 141
    of Alice 83
    superflatness (Murakami) 84
    tangping ('lying flat') 149–152
Foley, Caroline 141
Freddo *see* Nietzsche, Friedrich
futurism
    reproductive (Edelman) 86
fuwafuwa 30, 115

G

Garton, Vincent 69
gender 33, 93, 108, 169–171
    aegyo and 92
    anime girls and 39
    egg and 65
    euphoria 124
    genetics and 169
    hermaphroditism and 90
    indeterminate, of cute objects 90
    in manga and anime 114, 119
    kawaii and 31–32, 116
    moé and 145–147
    reassignment 102
    shōjo and 113, 118, 119
    transition 65, 102, 124–125
    Young-Girl and 129–130, 137
genetics 168, 185
    and adaptation 171
Geoffroy Saint Hilaire, Étienne 25–27, 63, 96–103, 104, 106, 107
geometry
    four-dimensional, Duchamp on 93
    Riemannian 141
    in Geoffroy 98
Gestalt
    Lorenz on 177
girl
    as affect (Nguyen) 115
    as trap (Deleuze and Guattari) 108
    as verb 112
    beautiful fighting 116–117, 141–142
    becoming- 24
    girldick 102
    girldinner 20

216

girlstack (Quicho) 115
see also shōjo, Young-Girl
Goddard, Jean-Christophe 107
Goethe, Johann Wolfgang von 107
Gould, Stephen J. 76
Grelet, Gilles 50, 110–111
Griaule, Marcel 60
Guattari, Félix 50, 51, 123
GUI (graphical user interface) 76
guilt 39, 157–158
gyaru 118

H
hands 76, 95
and paws 24–25
Harris, Daniel 77–78, 163
Heidegger, Martin 132
Heinroth, Oskar 176
hermaphrodite, hermaphroditism 18, 20, 88–90
heterogenesis 90
hirahira 30, 115
Honda, Toru 23, 143, 146, 148
Horikiri, Naoto 118
Howie, Elizabeth 84
Humpty-Dumpty 54, 80, 82
hyperstition 110, 124

I
Idea 1, 15, 18, 44, 162, 186, 190
ideaesthesia 75
identification
and desire 94
identity 33, 39, 158
and guilt 157–158
images 20, 36, 39, 119, 144, 147, 151, 155
in Japan vs. the West 147
inarticulacy 80–81, 95

in poetry 78
inauthenticity 164, 165
of Young-Girl 136
inducers 56
parents as 86
infantility, infantilisation 30, 43, 75, 81, 91, 116, 123
infants 73–74, 75, 114, 172–174, 175, 182, 183, 186
information theory 179
inhuman 5, 38, 40, 80
database sexuality as 40
moé as 38, 145
initiation 53–54, 65, 67, 124
innate releasing mechanisms (Lorenz) 176, 177
instinct
in Lorenz 176–178
vs institution (Deleuze) 169–170
institution 50, 124
vs instinct (Deleuze) 169–170
intelligence 12, 181
intensification 16, 17, 18, 43, 187, 188, 190
intensity 4, 6, 16, 66, 110, 157, 190
BwO as map of 59, 61, 64
Mark Fisher on 16
virtual body and 93
zero 27
interiority 13, 14, 20, 33
internet 5
in China 79
irreversibility 160

J
Japan 78, 81, 122–123, 142
Guattari on 123
history of kawaii in 114, 117
history of shōjo in 112–114

Jung, Carl Gustav 68, 177

K

Kant, Immanuel 59, 161
Katak 80
kawaii 12, 31–32, 70, 82, 95,
    115–116, 118
    infantility and 75
    shōjo and 114–115
    burriko and 81
    Guattari on 123
    qualities of 82
Kawasaki, Satoshi 107
Kewpie 80
Kindchenschema (Lorenz) 73, 74,
    75, 164, 173, 174, 175, 187, 188
kittens
    and mittens 95
Klein bottle 20, 92
Konior, Bogna 144, 157, 190, 191

L

Lacan, Jacques 92
lalangue 81
Land, Nick 68, 69, 158, 163
language 10–11, 80, 83
    acquisition of 181–182, 182
Last Men 4, 30
latent space 30, 100, 152, 190
Lavery, Grace 65
Levinson, Stephen 180–181
lines 106, 144, 155, 160
lines of flight 16, 17, 158
lolicon 122
Long Chu, Andrea 130
Lorenz, Konrad 11, 16, 73, 74, 164,
    173, 176–180, 188
love 7, 18, 45, 49
    2D 150, 153, 158
        courtly love and 143

supernormal and 153
Hayao Miyazaki and 141
relationship to reality
    147–148
    Honda Toru on 148
accelerationism as 6
database 38–39
hermaphroditism and 89
Lovecraft, H.P. 53, 66–67
Lunn Flies into the Wind 144

M

Mackay, Robin 85
Man 24, 66, 86
manga 76, 78, 119, 147, 148, 171
    Guattari on 123
    kawaii and 114–115
    representation and 147
    shōjo 114–116
mania
    and writing 50
market 37, 164, 187, 188, 190
    and moé 37
    black 124
Marx, Karl 140
masochism 15
Massumi, Brian 50
maturity 32, 46, 123
May, Simon 71
McGroot, Adolph 137
memory
    countermemory 160
    phylogenetic 26
    releasers and 177
meng 12, 76
Merish, Lori 77
Meta-nomad 70
Mickey Mouse 11
misogyny
    McGroot on 138

in Tiqqun 126–129, 139–140
mittens
    kittens and 95
Miyazaki, Hayao 75, 141
moé 36–40, 144, 144–147, 150,
    154, 155, 188
    cuteness and 145
    desire and 155
    music and 155
    partial objects and 37, 38, 154
    supernormality and 156
moé-elements 37–39, 79, 115
    abstraction and 156
Morinaga Takuro 35
morphogenesis 56–58
morphogenetic potential (Dalcq)
    57
morphology
    vs. physiology, in Cuvier and
        Geoffroy 98, 101–100
Morreall, John 165–167, 172–174
Moynihan, Thomas 104
multimodality 71, 75, 190
    of moé 38
Murakami, Takashi 84
Myers, Rhea 70, 84
myth 53–54, 60, 64, 65, 66
    Dogon 60–63
    Eliade on 63

N
n1x 69
nails 95
narcissism 120
natural selection 167, 168, 180,
    199 see also evolution
nature 25–26, 32, 43, 101, 102,
    124, 153, 172, 182, 187
    emergence of cute within 187
    in Geoffroy and Cuvier 102

programmability of 153
necrophilia 77
Neon Genesis Evangelion 156
Ngai, Sianne 78
Nietzsche, Friedrich 6, 24, 51, 68,
    148, 151, 157–158
nijikon 36, 146
nonsense 88
nostalgia
    and shōjo 112, 121
    for nature 153
nurture 16, 174, 182

O
object
    and kawaii 115
    and subject 10, 42, 158
    problematic 1
    cute 18, 21, 42, 43, 64, 75,
        77–78, 90, 121, 163, 183
    partial 38, 39, 153–154, 156,
        171
        moé-elements as 37, 38
    self-objectification 4, 20–21,
        31
    vs. process 156, 161–163
O'Neill, Rose 80
organism, organs 96, 98, 101,
    160, 161
    time and 64
    database and 60
    gender and 108
    development of, in
        embryology 55, 56
otaku 37, 39, 142, 143, 145, 148,
    150, 188
    culture of 154
    moé and 153
    shōjo and 120, 121–123
    tangping and 150–151

Ōtsuka, Eiji 119
oxymorons 87, 95

P
pain 10, 71
Panda and the Magic Serpent 141
parenting, parents 66, 86
    alloparenting 181–183
partial object *see* object
passivity 51, 137
    Morreall on 166
    Tiqqun on 129, 132, 135, 140
    consumerist 44
    denpa and 143
    of the Young-Girl 135
    see also submission, surrender
paws
    hands and 24
penetration 13, 14
people-to-come 151
perversion 7, 36, 67
phallus 13
photography
    fashion and 149
Piveteau, Jean 101
plane 141, 149
    of composition (Geoffroy) 26, 97–98, 100, 102, 106
    of consistency 125
Plant, Sadie 69, 85, 86
plasticity 33
    of behaviour 169–171
plushies 51, 152
    cthuloid type 68
poetry 78
Poincaré, Henri 141
pointedness, poignancy 10, 14, 71, 87, 95

politics
    activism 79
    McGroot on 137–138
    sociobiology and 167
Ponyo 75
possession *see* demons
postmodernity 5, 79, 156
pragmatism 33
problem, problematic 1, 42, 162, 190
propaganda 80
pyramids 11, 103

Q
quasiphonic particles 80–79
Quicho, Alex 92, 130
QWERTY 25

R
racism 85
reality 31, 32, 36–37, 103, 124, 147
    fantasy and 36
    fiction and 36, 147, 160
regression 5, 27, 44, 68, 100
    Jung on 68
releasers, releasing stimuli (Lorenz, Tinbergen) 16, 74, 164, 165, 173, 178–180, 184, 188
    moé-elements as 38
representation 60, 66, 81, 109, 147–148, 154, 156
    in manga and anime 147
reproduction 15, 16, 42, 44, 85–86, 138, 159
    shōjo and 119
    social 46
    Young-Girl and 135, 136
resentment 126, 158
responsibility 7, 158
revolution 5, 68

and desire 68, 157
riajuu 36
rigging 30, 33, 110, 111, 115
Rilke, Rainer Maria 45
ritual 54, 62, 64, 160
Robertson, Jennifer 119
Ruyer, Raymond 58

S
sā jiāo 81
Sanders, John T. 165–167,
  172–174, 182
schizophrenia 164
Sélavy, Rrose 93
self-objectification *see* object
seriousness 4, 6, 46, 83
sex 15, 42, 161–160
  evolution and 169
  moé and 35–36
  simulation and 85
  Ballard on 84
  cute (Harris) 77
  in Geoffroy 102
  simulation of 85
sexting 144, 157
sexuality 17, 37, 39, 42, 142, 187
  and AI 190
  and evolution 152
  and supernormality 152
  animal vs human, Deleuze on
    85
  asexuality
    and moé 146
  database 40
  drawn 36, 142
  fictosexuality 146
  of moé 38–39, 40, 40–44
  of shōjo 120
shame 32, 39, 140, 158–157, 158,
  159
  and autophilia 94

shamelessness 159
sharpness *see* pointedness,
  poignancy
Shin, Shangah 94
shōjo 30–32, 83, 112–123
  Alice and 83
  Bruno as 83
  manga 145
  as scapegoat 117, 121
signs
  shōjo as 113, 119
  sign stimuli (Tinbergen)
    178–180
  Dogon 62
  moé and 37–38
Singleton, Benedict 124
singularity 3, 52, 60
skins 92
skirts 24, 25
  go spinny 94
slime 68
snuggling 13
sociality 178–179, 181–183
social media 31, 76
  and flatmaxxing 149
sociobiology 40, 166–170
softness 3, 32
space 59, 61–62
  Japanese vs Western 147, 151
Spectacle 131, 135, 139
speech 80, 81, 83, 95
  baby talk 80–81, 91
Srnicek, Nick 69
subject 171
  capitalism and 132
  commodity and 166
  fiction and 147
  girl 115
  moé and 146
  object and 77, 158
  time and 75

shōjo 112, 113
Young-Girl 140
sublimation 25
submission, submissiveness 4, 16, 20, 46, 81, 138 *see also* surrender, passivity
superficiality 4, 13–15, 110, 125 *see also* flatness
superflat *see* flatness
supernormal, supernormalisation 11, 16, 17, 44, 153–155, 164, 185
moé and 38, 156
abstraction and 156
surrender 3, 5, 6, 46 *see also* submission, passivity
surrogacy 90, 184, 185, 187
Sutcliffe, Peter 137–138
swarm, swarming 31, 33, 40

T

Tamaki, Saitō 35–36, 116–115, 147
tangping *see* flatness
technology 5, 16, 52, 85, 110, 125, 148, 159–160, 170, 191
and supernormality 16
as egg-proxy 125
teddy bears 77, 185
teratology 98, 106
TikTok 80
time, temporality 26, 39, 75, 162
anatomy and, in Geoffroy 98
heterochrony 57, 175
myth and 62, 63
the egg and 64
the transcendental and, Nick Land on 162
Tinbergen, Nikolaas 11, 16, 172, 177–178, 184
Tiqqun 35, 112, 117, 118, 120, 121, 126–141

topology 13–14, 20, 56, 58, in Geoffroy 98, 100–101
transcendental 161–162
accelerationism and 100
empirical and 107
transformation 6, 26, 27, 30, 43, 52, 53, 56, 63, 65, 97, 100, 124, 146, 159
transgenderism 65–66, 102, 124–125
transgression 17
trap
evolutionary 186
girl as 108
trauma
and moé (Saitō Tamaki) 142
Treat, John Whittier 121
tummy
catboy 25
tungsten-carbide, of Capital 19

V

virtual, virtuality 26, 37, 46–47, 59, 75, 100, 109–110, 146
accelerationism and 27
body *see* body, virtual
moé and 146–147
Nick Land on 163
Von Baer, Ernst 54
Von Uexküll, Jakob Johann 176
vore 19–21

W

waifu 39
Watts, Natalie Terezi Rei 109
weaponisation 80
Williams, Alex 69
women 17, 115, 117, 129–132, 135
and capital 130–132

words 9, 12, 72, 82
writing 49

X
Xenofeminism 69

Y
yaoi 38
Yoshimoto, Takaaki 119
Young-Girl (Tiqqun) 112, 121,
    126–140, 149

Z
zero 1, 46–47
Zuckerman, Ethan 79